An Uphill Journey:
One Small Church's
Journey to Revitalization

Dr. Brian Nall

Brian Nall

ISBN: 0-9907816-8-2

ISBN-13: 978-0-9907816-8-4

DEDICATION

To the Family of Faith who are Ferris Hill
For letting your life and our journey be a story God would
read to the world.

To my family
For your unending love and encouragement.

To Baleigh and Elijah
You are the best kids in the world. I could not be prouder.

To my wife Candace
This book and this journey would not exist without you.
I love You!

To God be the Glory!

WHAT OTHERS ARE SAYING

Brian Nall gives us an honest and helpful story of revitalization. While the author says he speaks as a small church pastor to small church pastor, the nuts and bolts in the book will help any church be better. Be prepared to be challenged and given practical tools when you read An Uphill Journey!

Dr. Ted Traylor,
Senior Pastor of Olive Baptist Church
Pensacola, FL

An Uphill Journey reminds us that revitalization can happen anywhere, with any size church. Brian provides practical advice that not only encourages readers, but also equips them with the principles needed to bring about a God sized change in their own church context. Any pastor or lay leader frustrated with stagnation in their church would benefit from the story of Ferris Hill.

Dr. Will Rushing
Pastor of Woodward Avenue Baptist Church
Muscle Shoals, AL

This is a refreshing read about revitalization for pastors of smaller churches, which are by far the norm. I genuinely enjoyed walking down the pastoral path with Dr. Nall because of his transparency, pragmatism and contagious faith.

Dr. Mark Dance
Director of Lifeway Pastors
Lifeway Christian Resources

Dr. Nall, from a pastor's perspective, has written a valuable, well principled, book that is a living example for leading a church to revitalization. This work was done in a local congregation, which makes it a great resource, with end of the chapter questions that will aid the reader in personal application.

Rev. Chip Fox
Director of Missions for the Santa Rosa Baptist
Association (Santa Rosa County Florida)

Dr. Brian Nall has written a pragmatic and useful resource for Pastors and church leaders in all size congregations. The insights and transparency of one pastor's ministry challenges to others is helpful and challenging. The reflections at the conclusion of each chapter invite the reader to engage personally in the revitalization needs of the congregation they lead. Thank you Brian for your authentic leadership and ministry impact as you lead Ferris Hill to become the church that reaches UP, reaches OUT, and reaches IN. You'll be glad you took the time to read this book!

Lewis Miller
Regional Catalyst
Florida Baptist Convention

TABLE OF CONTENTS

ACKNOWLEDGMENTS

Like most pastors who attend church-based conferences, I usually sit under the instruction of the mega-church leaders. I am thankful for their influence, but I also realize that their example can be intimidating. Most of us are in small churches. (At the time I am writing, the church I am pastoring is knocking on the door of 200 in attendance.) It can be tempting to embrace the mindset that we can't make a meaningful impact until we reach the "mega" level. I reject that thought. This book is written to the small church by a small church pastor to say, "don't wait."

Ten years ago when I arrived at Ferris Hill, I am not sure who was more nervous – them or me. Thank you Ferris Hill for your prayers and patience as we grow together to reach our community and beyond. So many contributed to our turnaround as a church: to the FHBC brainstorming team who shared their personal stories and insights for this book, for the staff and family of faith, past and present, who have poured their blood, sweat, tears and prayers in to this work God has given us. Thank you Lauren Sutton for your editing services.

The city of Milton and Santa Rosa County have embraced our church as much as we have sought to embrace them. Thank you for continually opening your arms to us as we pursue to BE the church.

FORWARD

I have read hundreds of books on church revitalization and renewal. If I was asked to pick one for the small church in America struggling to keeps its doors open and minister to the community, it would be this book! You will want to read of this Church Revitalizer's journey to revitalize a dying church! This is the book for the majority of us who do not pastor a mega church. You have heard the old statistic over and over again: more people in America attend a large church; yet there are more small churches in America. Demographic agencies are the first to remind all of us that the fastest growing religious segment in all of America is the none's. Those with no religious affiliation. Dr. Brian Nall challenges and reminds us that all churches, both large and small have much room for improvement. To address this need, more strong churches are needed. This last phrase is a two-fold emphasis. *More* strong churches are needed; thus, church planting efforts must be embraced in countless untapped corners of our communities. Furthermore, *strong* churches are needed; thus, church revitalization efforts must also be embraced in the vast thousands of churches that already exist.

Uphill Journey is the story of "how" a small church grew strong and stable. Notice I didn't say, grew large. Brian Nall captures the journey of how his small church embraced biblical principles to make a transforming impact upon one of the fastest growing counties in Florida. Since most pastors in America have under 200 in attendance, most pastors can relate to this book. Brian captures the who, the why and the how that helped this once declining, long-established church, turn the revitalization corner. As you will see, this was not easy, revitalization of a dying church is never an easy task. This book needs to be read by laymen as well as pastors of small churches. It can save you from rapid decline and eventual death.

Thankfully, many books and conferences have been developed toward both the "more" and the "strong" in recent years. But there is still much work to be done for the "small" or "declining." That brings us to the "how." Fifty years from now, if the Lord tarries, those who are just getting involved in church revitalization will be reading of this pastor's journey up the hill and over the hill towards a glorious future. Nall's journey tells of God's story to turn around his church. You would be wise to draw from his wisdom in the crossing over from decline to vital health. If you are open to drawing the strength and wise principles from *Uphill Journey* it can fuel your church's future and passage towards recreating a healthy church.

Tom Cheyney, Founder & Directional Leader
Renovate National Church Revitalization Conference

INTRODUCTION
A NEW JOURNEY ON A FAMILIAR ROAD

It was another mild Saturday afternoon in February – one of those times of year in Florida when you wear shorts one day and a heavy coat the next. I was traveling to the city of Milton on a stretch of Highway 90 that I had traveled numerous times being a native of the Panhandle. Over my then twenty-eight years, I had crisscrossed this stretch of road with my grandfather heading up to one of his secret fishing holes; with my parents visiting family; and with the youth groups I had pastored for nearly ten years while taking them tubing. (Later I learned Milton was "the Canoe Capital of Florida"). But this trip was different.

I was heading only twenty-one miles from where my wife Candace and I lived with Baleigh, our fifteen-month-old daughter, to meet the Pastor Search Team of Ferris Hill Baptist Church. As I maneuvered through traffic in my silver 2002 Ford Escort ZX2[1], I seemed to have a thousand questions rushing through my mind: How did this church get my resume? What questions did I need to ask? What questions did I hope *they* would ask? Are there topics I shouldn't ask? What will they "forget" to tell me? Why was I needed to pastor a church in this area when it seemed like the county already had one on every corner? Literally! Were they ready for me? Was I ready for this?

---

[1]This was a "trade" with my wife when she was "great with child." At 6'3", I learned the art of rolling in and out of cars.

By then, in 2006, I already finished my thirteenth year of ministry. I surrendered to ministry during my sophomore year of high school and was licensed a few months after graduation. At that time, I felt God steering my life to be a life-long Student Pastor. Senior Pastor had not been on my radar. Leading and teaching while in high school and my first year of college seemed to get my feet wet to ministry. By the time I started studying at the University of Mobile I was ready to take on the youth of America. And for two and a half years I attempted to mold young lives in the quaint town of Citronelle, Alabama in my first full-time ministry position. I poured my time into everything student ministry and tried not to leave too many scars upon the students as I learned from my frequent mistakes. (If any of those students or parents are reading this, "I'm sorry.")

Wrapping up my tenure in Citronelle with ministry ordination, days in Alabama soon became days in Louisiana as I moved to New Orleans to get my long-planned seminary education underway. After a year of living on campus and assisting a couple of local ministries, I came back home to Pensacola to spend my summer supply preaching. The Director of Missions for the Baptist Association welcomed me eagerly as he told me the average age of his supply preachers was eighty.

A week into my summer of preaching I received a call from a local pastor who needed an interim youth pastor for the summer. I told him I could give him eight weeks until I needed to return to New Orleans. God had other plans. By late July the church asked if I would come on staff as their permanent part-time youth minister. Sensing God in the middle of it, plus knowing I could dizzyingly conquer the logistics of commuting, I agreed. For the next nine months I commuted weekly, some weeks multiple times, between Pensacola and New Orleans – 187 miles one way. When I wasn't in class I was writing small group material, preparing to train cell group leaders who met on their respective nights when I was away at school, and leading a Saturday night youth service. The months flew by with much growth and excitement – especially since I would be getting married at the end of the school year.

By the end of the next semester I was finishing my schooling through independent study and serving at the church full-time. A week after Candace and I returned from our honeymoon, the Senior Pastor left to be the new Director of Missions in the Association. His departure left me with the task of not only youth ministry, but pastoring the North Campus (which met in an active funeral home and could be a whole other book in itself), overseeing the Recreation Ministry, Missions Ministry and coordinating responsibilities with our Interim Pastor who traveled in from out of town for Sunday responsibilities.

Over the next five years, with the expectations from the Senior Pastor and other expectations I placed on myself, my ministry responsibilities increased. I greatly enjoyed the administration needs of ministry, and I was soon moved to be the Executive Pastor with all the other ministries and staff under my purview. From early on, I seemed to get a ministry rush from aligning all the various components of ministry (people, facilities, community, policy) and moving them all in a singular direction in order to accomplish a God-led vision. As I served and led the church through all these changes, I felt God maneuvering me to serve Him in a different capacity. I sensed God laying the foundation to be a Senior Pastor. Though I had great clarity about this new direction, I was uncertain about what to do next as I have never submitted my resume to a church without first being asked. This uncertainty was NOT comfortable. As I have come to discover through repeated occurrences, emotional discomfort often precedes divine direction.

God's divine direction led me to that familiar road in Milton. As I got closer to where I thought was my turn into Ferris Hill, my eyes looked frantically for church signage. I spotted the marquee and turned onto the tree-covered road. I proceeded cautiously for about 200 yards seeing neither church nor sign and wondering if I should have packed a flare. After a quarter mile, I came to a stop sign, still no church. I spotted a little worn out painted sign under the overgrowth of a nearby hedge. (Years later we would replace this sign after coordinating with city, county, and state officials, plus a nearby a home owner, to get location approval since the roads are near a state-run bike trail). I proceeded east one more block and joyfully found the tucked-away church campus with its corner sign, beyond well-used, having several letters weathered off. Now, where to park?

I saw a few cars tucked into the north side of the parking lot and took my chances. John, the chairman of the team, greeted me on the sidewalk and escorted me into what I came to discover was the Pastor's office where the rest of the team had already assembled. The meeting went as one would expect – testimony, call to ministry, philosophy of ministry, and several minutes of Q&A. During this time the team shared their hopes but became vulnerable and shared their hurts as well.

Their list of hurts was not short. It actually grew with every passing conversation. After our time in the office, the team gave me a tour of the facility. One team member eagerly inquired as to how long did I think it would take to fill up the sanctuary again as it had been "in the good ol' days." As we walked, trying not to get lost in the maze of hallways, I began to make a mental to-do list for the aging facility, comparing it to my current church's facility that was only twenty-five years old.

I did have some requests if I were to come: One, the Pastor's office door had to have a window in it.[2] Two, the sleeper-sofa in the Pastor's office that part of the team was sitting on had to go.[3] Three, may I have a computer? They gladly agreed to take care of number one and two but needed to wait until a business meeting to consider number three. It passed,

---

[2] I desired to have an office environment that was properly transparent – for my protection as well because of the church history they shared.

[3] I realize that ministry can be tiring and there are moments when you can put in more hours than you desire, but I preferred to sleep at home. Perhaps I'm weird.

and I had a computer on my first day. The first meeting led to a second one where I did the standard preaching at a nearby church. That led to the "view of a call" day in early March.

Ferris Hill Baptist Church birthed into the ecclesiastical world in the mid 1940's as an intentional plant from Milton First Baptist. The intent was to have a church for the blue collar folks who might not feel comfortable at a "First"-style church. The high point, the good old days, was in the mid 1960's. But since that time, heartache seemed to define the church more than anything else. In the years ahead, I met hundreds of people who "used to go" to Ferris Hill. Split after split and one painful moment after another left a group of senior adults, who I affectionately referred to as "the survivors", and "the bus kids" who rode each week as the church continued to operate a bus ministry begun in the early 1970's. But there was practically no middle generation. I could count on one hand the number of people between ages 25-55.

On the "view of a call" Sunday, I was pleased to see the church almost filled – something that wouldn't happen again for a while. Dressed in my best suit (I was the only person wearing one), I preached on the difference between committing to God and surrendering to God. I used a visual aid which would give a fair warning of the endless unconventional teaching aids I would unleash in the years to come. When the time for Q&A came for the whole church, there was only one question: "What do you think about women on staff?" After answering satisfactorily, I filled a few more minutes with what I *thought* needed to be shared at a time like this before our family was dismissed for the vote – they approved. It was time to get to work.

The pages that follow record our journey.

CHAPTER 1
NUTS AND BOLTS, PART 1

After 70 years in exile, God's people were released to return to their promised land. The return came in three different waves. Zerubbabel led 50,000 people back in c. 525B.C.-focusing first on the foundation of the temple (Ezra 2-3). Ezra came later with the second wave-focusing on establishing the law and traditions (c. 458 B.C.; Ezra 7-8). Finally, Nehemiah returned in c. 444B.C. with his focus upon rebuilding the walls and gates (Nehemiah 1-7). Each leader was focused upon a specific phase that was integral to the completion of the overall project. There was order. Not everything was focused on simultaneously. There were hiccups and set-backs. There were lessons learned; lessons that we can still learn from in order to strengthen churches today.

In this chapter, and then part two in chapter 5, you will read the principles that have shaped the faith family of FHBC and our pursuit of revitalization. If you only read these two chapters and don't get to how the story unfolded for us, that's fine. My intention is not for you to copy us. My desire is for you to use the principles that guided us in order to develop a ministry framework for your own revitalization, or for a new launch that you can apply within the ministry context God has placed you.

Principle #1 – The Bible is the primary driver.

The car industry is quickly pursuing the self-driving car. A recent California newspaper showed a couple of police officers who were quite surprised to stop a car that had no driver.[4] Self-driving, or should it be called "non-self-driving," is considered adventurous in the automotive industry, but it is destructive within the church. No church will reach their God-preferred future with a hands-off approach, letting "come what may" be the mantra.

Chasing after the latest success strategy or most creative idea that surfaces is a frequent ministry temptation for me. It may be for you as well. We can have these hope-filled unspoken prayers, "maybe this will be the one that works." Though such a temptation might be knocking on your office door, don't open it. Consider for a moment: have you used the Bible to be what drives, tangibly mobilizes, your church towards God's preferred future? While strategies and success stories can be an aid, let the Bible be the driver. Let me encourage you to make it your pastoral goal to bring the Bible off the page and into the lives of your people. The writer of Hebrews wrote that the Bible is "living and active" (Heb. 4:12). As a pastor or church leader and ecclesiastical equipper, treat the Bible as such. Study the scriptures faithfully, with proper exegetics, and prayerfully lead your people to bring it to life in their life.

Consider, what would such a shift look like in your ministry for the Bible to be the primary tool to

---

[4] http://www.cbc.ca/news/business/google-self-driving-car-slow-1.3318196

shape your church? Really. How could you position your church to be without need among the people (Acts 4:35)? How could you focus your church so it revolved itself *only* around prayer, fellowship, breaking of bread together and the study and application of God's word (Acts 2)? While you might agree with this in theory and are currently shouting out "duh", take a moment to reflect on what *is* currently driving the direction of your church – Robert's Rules of Order, traditions of the past, the preferences of a few loud or influential voices, what's broke, the ideas of a leader you greatly respect, a recent book you read, business principles? After you answer that question, how would those you lead respond to such a question? Can those in your church easily connect your ministry endeavors to scripture? If we are honest, we might find that the practical outworking of our ministry doesn't reflect what we state are our convictions.

Notice my word choice, "Bring the Bible to life." I didn't say, "Bring it to understanding." If only understanding (mental ascent) is the primary goal, your church will fall short of revitalization. Scripture is clear that followers of Jesus obey His commands (1 John 2:1-6; John 15:14). In response, as you come across expectations God has for His followers, ensure such ministries and values are practiced in your church. (Or at least make note of them so you have a list of the direction you want to head). Obviously, there are hundreds of biblical guides to follow. Because of their number we can get overwhelmed and never begin. Resist. Get a notepad and jot down five biblical expectations God has for HIS church. Where do you see those biblical expectations applied in your church? Can your people clearly, quickly and easily connect the dots between the ministry -"what" and the biblical- "why?"

Let me encourage you to commit to biblical priority. Plan biblical priority. Lead your staff meetings, deacon meetings, church council meetings, and committees/teams according to biblical priority. Additionally, as you study, both in personal faith practice and preparing for the corporate setting, reflect on how a particular passage could come to life in your context. If you have ministries that you cannot easily, with exegetical integrity, align with the biblical examples, commands and values, stop them. It doesn't make sense to give energy and resources to something God, who we claim to follow and worship, neither expects nor demands.

A repeated principle I have held up for our people: "if I seek to lead us to do something that is not in scripture, call me on it publicly." Could that mean we have a lean ministry list? Yes. But we will then be faithful in a few essential items instead of exhausted in the unnecessary. You will be surprised by the depth of health that will come to your church as you make scripture the primary driver.

To Consider:
1   How clearly is the Bible shaping how I lead my church? Where could I improve?
2   How am I using the Bible to transform our church instead of only inform our church?

Principle #2 (or 1.2) – Application Surpasses Information

Luke was one of our 30-somethings who had an extensive church testimony. As we chatted over lunch, he recounted his story: plugged in here, left there, plus a few in and out of's mixed in. And the church timeline continued. I turned the conversation to his faith testimony. (Be sure to know the difference between a faith testimony and a church testimony). He politely explained his struggle. As he sat under my teaching each week, he confessed that he was having to completely re-examine his faith, his relationship to Jesus, and the purpose of the Bible. The reason? For all his church life no one ever told him he was to actually *do* anything with the Bible other than understand and respect it. He said as I was leading our church to apply the Bible he was now having to look at the Bible in a whole different way and wasn't sure anymore. His response left me both shocked and saddened.

The Epistle of James says we are to be "doers of the word" (Jms. 1:27). John writes a defining marker of a disciple is one who "does what He commands" and "walks as Jesus walked" (1 Jn. 2:6). Cover to cover the Bible reaffirms people who encountered God and then had to do something in response to that encounter (e.g. Abraham, Moses, Elisha). Their response was not to memorize the encounter and then form a committee to better understand it. The goal was application.

To embrace Christ is not to merely gain intellectual understanding of the divine or the historical. Instead, it is to live it out through the enabling and indwelling power of the Holy Spirit. Leading a church toward revitalization involves leading them beyond the intellectual understanding of the Bible and toward making concrete application within their own life and the world around them. This isn't always easy to pull off. As a pastor, it is easy to say, "Here you go" and then expect everyone to know how to run with the application. In my twenty-plus years of ministry, those who naturally "run with it" are few and far between. Psychologists and counselors say it takes more cognitive ability to move from concrete thinking (information) to abstract thinking (personal application). As pastor/teacher/equipper, it is my responsibility to help connect the dots; set the stage that would aid in biblical application (which is the true mark of a disciple).

After writing out my teaching manuscript for Sunday, I often sit back and picture our Worship Center. I imagine the faces I will teach to in a few days and then ask, "What would it look like for _____ to apply this." I then adjust the wording of illustrations or add in specific suggestions for application that would connect with those who will be recipients. I am also careful to avoid phrases such as, "the *familiar* story of...", or "as you know" as several adults just beginning their faith journey have expressed they have never heard of a book/letter, verse, or biblical account.

While my ability to give precise application is inadequate (I'm not the omniscient Holy Spirit), I at least want to be headed in the right direction. My goal is that it will then easier for those who hear to take the next step to apply. Sure, it takes more effort on my part, but it is more than worth it when I hear stories of application in the days that follow. In your tireless work of biblical teaching, prioritize application.

To Consider:

1   Where could the listener go in the next 3 days to apply what I have just taught?
2   If God is going to say, "Well done" to the listener, according to the portion of the Bible I have just taught them, what exactly might they have done?

Principle #3 – Know What's Important

You probably have your own horror stories of church business meetings gone badly: someone didn't approve the motion to purchase more toilet paper, should we purchase pew Bibles with or without maps, should we pay to tune the piano. I am thankful that we have not faced the previous examples at Ferris Hill, but I'm sure some of you have. The point is that you, as the under-shepherd of your flock, must know God's word well so that you can know which issues are essential to put up a fight for and which are not. I have seen many pastors falter in revitalization because they sought to make *every* idea that is voiced an essential issue only to "die" in the end on the unimportant and never experience revitalization and biblical church health.

Dr. Taylor was one of my professors at the University of Mobile (Go Rams!). In my senior year, he told a group of us preacher boys, "Know the few things in life and ministry that are most sacred; everything else, take with a grain of salt and know how to laugh at yourself." That piece of advice has stuck with me all these years later.

Whenever someone makes a ministry recommendation, I evaluate how it fits into the overall direction God has given us. Is it biblical? Does this align with what God has called us to? Will following this recommendation hinder or confuse the mission? The clear majority of the time the request is not a make or break issue and nothing worth losing sleep over. Taking time to listen, heeding ideas and conceding your preferences, helps people to feel valued for shaping and contributing to the life of the church (Which is essential since we are all the body and everyone is needed.) No matter what the recommendation is, there are some issues that I will not move on. One of those issues is the foundation of our music.

I have been clear that the music during our church gatherings will always be based on the biblical text we are embracing that day. I usually get my teaching plan to our worship leader weeks ahead of time. He then knows to pick songs that align with the biblical text. It makes no difference to me if the songs were written 150 years ago or 10 minutes ago. God has used people across multiple generations to communicate His truths. It makes no difference to me as long as they are biblically related and "christologically clear" (we made this term up); meaning, songs where there is no doubt Christ Jesus is the subject instead of vague references to something beyond. We are happy to incorporate all textually relevant songs as best as our abilities will permit. We will not, however, just plug in songs that make us feel good or for the sake of "it is my favorite one."

Appropriately chosen songs even assist in the understanding and application of scripture- three sermon points might not be remembered but song verses may. Because we build everything in our church on scripture, I don't move on this principle. Has this ruffled some feathers along the way? Sure. There will always be battles between honoring personal preferences and prioritizing God and His word.

In church revitalization as in the Kenny Rogers song (though not condoning gambling) – "you got to know when to hold 'em, know when to fold 'em, know when to walk away, know when to run…" Don't battle every issue. Know what is essential to the mission and lay down your leadership life for it. Everything else, let it go. Save your energy for what really matters.

To Consider:
1   Is what this person is desiring going to help or

> hinder the long term mission of the church God has given?
2   What are the few items that I will not negotiate? Everything else, is it worth a battle?

Principle #4 – Use the Community to Strengthen the Church

Pastors can have a superman complex. (There I said it.) Especially in the smaller-sized church without full-time staff assistance, we can feel the responsibility to leap the steeple in a single bound. Everyone is looking toward us, at least it feels this way, to have the answers that will lead the church and everyone's personal life toward their preferred future. And the answers are not just theological in nature. The questions range from evangelism, missions, building and grounds, finances, community engagement, and counseling to insurance, personnel, legal, flowers, automotive, bereavement and benevolence. But don't forget men's, women's, youth, location of diaper changing stations, and... There can be a sense of pride to say, "here is the answer, go ye therefore and complete." But is such an answer the *best* answer or just *your* answer. How often do you say, "I don't know?"

While pastors can have great wisdom, so do others. It takes a pastor exercising great humility and wisdom to know what they don't know and to defer to others. What can be even more frightening is what you don't know you don't know. Fortunately, God has placed others in your life that know what you don't and who see what you can't. For instance, the single mom on food stamps who knows the state of poverty in the community better than you, the power company representative who can give your church an energy audit to make recommendations, the mayor or city council members who see the needs of the city daily, the guidance counselor at the school who has a pulse on hundreds of families near you.

King David had "the men of Issachar who knew the times" (1 Chron. 12:32)-those with a pulse on what is happening today and not only how it "used to be." It is the skilled wise person who humbly holds today's newspaper in one hand and the Bible in the other. Sometimes the way we "know the times" is to know the *people* who know the times. Such people are all throughout your community and throughout your church. Meet them. Rely on them. Pray for and with them. Trust them. Develop a relationship with them. Let them be of assistance to you. The time will come when they need you.

To Consider:
1   What professional in our community could give advice to our struggle?
2   What organizations in our community could we partner with to ….?

Principle #5 – Model What You Expect

You are not yet who God ultimately wants you to be. Your church is not done becoming who God wants her to be. Since there is a gap between where we are and where we need to be, it is helpful for there to be a reference point. A plumb line to check against to evaluate where we are from where we need to be. Personally we have Jesus whose actions and attitude we are to emulate (Philippians 2:5); but many in the church, and even the broader community, look to you, like it or not, as their shepherd to be their point of spiritual and moral reference. As their shepherd-leader/ teacher-equipper it is our responsibility to demonstrate what is expected. Follow me as I follow Christ (1 Corinthians 11:1). To be the reference point of revitalized health between where they are and where they need to be. This requires us to both possess what it is God expects of a leader and Christ follower and then to demonstrate it, both publicly and privately (1 Timothy 4:16).

The leadership adage holds true – the people can go no further than their leader. As God leads your church to serve "the least of these", you need to be the first to get in the trenches. If you want people to take care of the campus, then don't pass a piece of litter without picking it up. If Sunday School is important, then attend a class yourself and share publicly what God is doing. If you want your church to engage the community and the nations, give them a living sermon in you. Will this stretch your personal comfort zone? You bet.

In 2008, with our transportation ministry working well, our children's department was growing faster than other departments. And since most of our

19

adult growth was coming from those who had never been in church before, we didn't have a pool of godly adults to pull from in order to teach our expanding children's classes. I considered other personnel options but only found one person-the person I saw when I looked in the mirror. Now, I need to confess, I love children (I have two), but children's ministry is not my natural affinity. However, the second graders needed a teacher, and I stepped in and adapted. They taught me a lot (especially about patience), and I hope I set a godly example and poured biblical truth into them along the way. After a year, another teacher was ready but this time the need shifted to our fourth and fifth graders. Here we go again.

For the next two years, I spent some time with these moldable pre-teens. Though at times inconvenient for other pastoral duties I needed to handle, I wouldn't have traded those years for anything. Now, those preteens are wrapping up their high school years and are the leaders in the student ministry. But without consciously realizing it (I was only told this later by one of our Senior Adults), I was sending a message that there was no job any of us should not be willing to step up and try. I was glad to be the illustration. At the time of this writing, I am leading a class for our 20-somethings, preparing to hand off the teaching reins once again.

Your church needs to confidently feel that you will never ask them to do something you aren't willing to do or currently doing yourself. Very few people can "get it" by just reading a policy or listening to a sermon. Your life is the loudest sermon anyone will ever hear. The pastor needs to serve as the picture of revitalization you hope the church to become.

To Consider:

1   How am I modeling what I am asking of my people?

2   Is there any area of ministry that I am communicating, "that is beneath me" or "I am not willing to…"

Principle #6 – Develop For the Future

As you look throughout your church, you might not see the people you need to fill current ministry gaps. I feel your pain. In recent years most of our church growth has come from those with little or no church background. I think I am on pretty solid ground that it is unwise to put a man as a deacon or Sunday School teacher who learned about Moses for the first time last week (James 3:1). It's not a good idea to add a person to your stewardship team who was released from prison last month. But there are people who could be leaders in the future. There are young men sitting in your church today who will make great deacons in five years. There are some older teens who can make great teachers in time but are diamonds in the rough today. What could you do to prepare your church to have healthy leaders in five or ten years?

Two areas we began to intentionally look to the future was in our Deacon and Sunday School ministry, and in time were able to see a harvest of new leaders emerge. Was there a season where the burden was heavier upon a few of us, yes? Are we yet where we want to be, no? Though it might have been easier to lure leaders from other churches, we didn't feel it was a good practice. We needed to take the responsibility to develop some people who in time would be ready to lead. This takes time. Meaning, if you don't like the burden you are currently experiencing, begin now to invest in others who can share the load in the future.

To Consider:

1   What young people do we have today whom we could intentionally invest in to lead tomorrow?

2   How can we develop our "diamonds in the rough?"

CHAPTER 2

MARCH 27 2006

Several events filled my first day behind the well-worn desk. I spent a few moments in the sanctuary praying for this opportunity ahead. (Though I did not know all that laid ahead, I did know I would fall flat on my face without prayer and divine strength.) After navigating through the maze of hallways from the sanctuary to my office (I only got lost once in the dark), I ordered a demographic study from North American Mission Board with the hope that I could get a better grasp on the 1, 3, and 5-mile radius of the surrounding area *I thought* I knew.[5] The report revealed that what I thought I knew was not the reality. According to the most recent census, 143 families living one mile from the church were at or below the poverty line. The number jumped to 703 families when I went out to three miles. I then read of the education rates, income factors, family dynamics, renting vs. home ownership and much more.[6]

This information didn't launch me into a tailspin of concern; rather, it served as a helpful source of information I could use to clarify and communicate where we needed to go and why. For instance, when I was later working through passages that dealt with the

---

[5] You can order your own demographic study at
https://www.namb.net/demographics-request

[6] Find out about your own community at
http://factfinder.census.gov

poor and needy, I could specifically share this number and then ask simply, "what biblical responsibility do we have as a follower of Jesus toward the 143 families one mile from where we sit?" Further, when selecting the right pew Bible we wanted to have in our worship center, I could ask church leaders what reliable translation of the Bible should we get in light of the average education level of our community. While I would get an updated demographic report after the next census, I returned often to that original report to shape and tangibly communicate the direction of our church. After the report on that first Monday, I made a list.

List Making

I live off of lists. Since childhood, my mother engrained list-making into my daily routine. Weekly chores and daily homework assignments became staple items on my lists: clean room, pester my sister, study for my math test, mow the grass and the like. But my list-making didn't stop with what I had *planned to* accomplish. If I accomplished something not on the list, I would often go back and *add it to* my list just so I could have the satisfaction of crossing it off. Can I get a witness? (Recently, I began to move all my to-do items immediately onto my calendar so I can schedule their accomplishment, so my list-making is greatly reduced. Love you mom.)

The first list I made would influence my leadership for several years. While the list was not etched in concrete, it did list the items I felt were essential to lead my long established, yet personally new, church toward health: computers with internet, staff, guidelines for the staff, financial policies and procedures, childcare policies and background checks for all workers, revised constitution and bylaws, updated campus, establishing a membership covenant. (Yes, this was week one. I didn't yet have a plan for week two). As you will read in the pages ahead, the accomplishment of this list was not an overnight undertaking. In fact, the last item on this opening list, membership covenant, would not be crossed off for nine years.

Leading a church toward revitalization is more than completing a task list. While part of revitalizing a church involves policies, vision and structure, the primary component is people. Therefore, my main focus was positioning the people, who *are* the church, for revitalization. I quickly realized it was not wise to lead at my preferred speed; rather, while keeping the overall ministry trajectory in mind, my speed of change was determined by prayer and what was at the border of our people's comfort zone. Also, some of the ministry items that I could not venture into because I needed more credibility – which can only come with time and trust. Speed of ministry and change were based off of relationship – vertically and horizontally. As any pastor knows, the process of revitalization creates a petri-dish for developing patience for the pastor. Let me share a first hurdle.

We asked our church to require background checks for everyone working with minors. I had been at the church about a year. During that time, I had done a good bit of reading on legal issues in church.[7] As the shepherd, I wanted to protect our people and also create a welcoming and secure environment for the young families who would come (background checks can be a good outreach tool). I finally found the company I wanted us to use for the background checks along with their templates for forms each person was to complete. But rushing forward, not embracing patience, I sped through the reading of the material and sent it out to be completed by our volunteers. Needless to say, I skipped the sentence that said we would be conducting credit checks and possibly taking urine samples. Can you imagine the response I got? My lack of patience delayed a needed work. I was in such a hurry to get it done, I didn't take the time to get it right. Thankfully, the church was gracious, allowed me to backtrack and clarify, and we moved forward.

Back to that first day…

In addition to the list making and data gathering, I began to ask myself a question: "If our church closed its doors, would the community care or notice?" I could never remember exactly where I read that quote but it stuck with me. And, based on what was soon told me, I didn't like the answer.

While I was prayer-walking the surrounding

---

[7] I strongly recommend Richard Hammar's Church Law and Tax Update (churchlawandtax.com) or David Gibbs and The Christian Law Association (www.christianlaw.org).

community during those first few weeks, I met some people in the community and asked them what they thought about our church and how we might be able to pray for and serve them. Several inquisitively asked me where the church was located. Sadly, I pointed to the big brick building about 300 yards away, standing there for fifty years. My to-do list got a little longer that day.

Asking the Right Question

I have discovered that questions tend to shape ministry more than proclamations. They just better be the right questions. In counseling, the right question can lead someone to open up when their emotional wall is building. In discipleship, the right question can move the stagnant Christ follower to a deeper level of obedience. In leading revitalization, the right question can inspire a faithful group of ministry survivors to dream again. The right question can open up ministry possibilities when conventional wisdom would say it's impossible.

Question-driven ministry fills the pages of the Bible. It's Nathan asking David if he knows who's guilty. It's Jesus asking Peter, "Who do you say that I am?" It's Peter asking Jesus, "Can I come to you on the water?" It's the hurter asking the wounded, "will you forgive me?"

For the first six months I asked a bunch of questions – partly because of ignorance and partly so I could just be a better pastor. (Our people still say I answer most of their questions with another question.)

I pulled out the church's last pictorial directory and, beginning that first day, went home to home getting to know the sheep in my new ministry fold.

At this point it might be helpful to know something about me. I'm an introvert. While public speaking and teaching fuels my ministry fire, my natural energy comes from shaping organizations, designing strategies and implementing one of my favorite verses, "everything should be done in a fitting and orderly way" (1 Cor. 14:40). I am not naturally drawn to spend time with people. I must be transparent and confess that social settings are draining. If given the option to hang out with someone or complete a project alone, I will choose the project. I have realized my relational bent and have to work hard to manage it in balance with the relational necessities of pastoring. My social preferences must not be an excuse to neglect ministry responsibilities. Relationships are essential to fulfill God's calling on my life and to lead the church to fulfill the work God has planned for her to do (Eph. 2:10). But an under-shepherd must know what is going on in the lives of the sheep, regardless of personality or preferences. Therefore, in leading and pastoring there are frequent moments when I have to "get over myself."

At each home I visited during those first six months, I entered with my list of questions. After covering the formalities and sharing my story, I proceeded with my big 5:

• What is your faith and ministry testimony?

- What is your favorite moment in the history of the church?

- What would you like to see our church do in the days ahead?

- What would be helpful for me to know as your pastor?

- How can I pray for you?

Since I didn't want the visit to feel formal, I memorized the questions ahead of time and made sure I memorized their answers. On numerous occasions, I would leave the visit only to pull around the corner to park and complete the little form I made for each home to record their answers. After gathering a stack of responses, I would look back through them to see if common themes emerged – despair, excitement, hope, watershed events. This simple tool helped me gain a better understanding and affection of my new church and the people I was blessed to pastor.

In the days ahead as God opened up doors for ministry opportunities in the church and the community, I was able to use their responses to make the connection as to how those opportunities were fulfilling a dream or desire the church had been keeping. Additionally, when I felt change was needed in a particular area, I looked back to their responses and used the burdens they shared to further fuel why we needed to move in a particular God-prompted direction.

So where does a pastor begin? Of all that I wrote down I began to ask: which item do I *want* to complete, do I *need* to complete, and which item must be done *first*. The answer is stacked.

My brother-in-law Andy is a mechanical engineer. He works as a contractor for a company that builds military ships. For hours he works with the designers and architects getting every detail in order. A lot of ideas are tossed out but not all will work, or should work. Then he moves to the ship yard to put the project from the paper into the water. Finally, he moves to another location where he oversees a lot of the "bugs" getting worked out before the ship is ready to advance and defend our freedom.

This same process happens in church revitalization. There are many hours you, the pastor or leader pursuing revitalization, will spend as a prayerful architect over the church. In private, many ideas can get tossed out, but not all work, nor should. The private work turns public when the church is mobilized to put the prayerfully-crafted plans into action- all with the understanding that this is work in process. We aren't perfect. We learn. We leave room for working out the kinks. (Thankfully God is patient in working out our kinks and doesn't chunk us when we mess up the first time.)

There were some times I worked behind the scenes on an item I knew was of less priority but needed some initial ground work. For instance, I arranged an introductory meeting with the city mayor during my second week to introduce myself and to see how I can pray for him and discover how he felt our church could best serve the community.[8] Publicly, there were more pressing issues within the church than meeting community leaders. From discovering the strained pastoral history, I discerned that restoring credibility and trust to the office of the pastor was of high importance if I was going to be the one who aided in moving them toward their preferred ecclesiastical future. But none of this is accomplished overnight. The commitment to revitalization is for the long-haul. That first day was a long one, but I remember being thankful yet excited for the unknown that God had in store. And with God's guidance and grace our desires would be realized.

Now for day two.

To Consider

1. What tool could you use to hear the personal story of each person in your church and get a grasp on their opinion of the church?
2. What do you see are the big items your church needs? Take a moment and write them down. What needs more work in private? What idea is ready to go public? Spend some time praying over them for priority and timing.
3. How's your patience level? How has your lack of

---

[8] I have routinely made it a practice to phone or email local government leaders to inquire as to how we could pray for them and if there is anyway our church could serve or be of assistance to them.

patience hindered your ministry? When has it helped?

4. What part of your personality, like being an introvert, do you need to keep in mind? If unsure, who could you ask to get an accurate assessment?

CHAPTER 3
CREATING MOVEMENT

Stagnation – ['stag, nat]: "to cease flow or move; to cease developing; become inactive or dull"

Running through the middle of our city is the Blackwater River. Known for its great fishing holes and cold water, this river is a favorite resource for sports enthusiasts, families, and serious outdoorsmen. One of the branches of the Blackwater River is Cold Water Creek. On more times that I can count, I have floated down this river on a canoe or tube with family and friends to defeat the humidity of Florida summers. The process is simple- paddle. The boundaries are clearly marked – the woods. The obstacles are numerous- fallen logs, protruding rocks and many other projectiles that are enemies of the preschool rapids. If you ever get caught, your progress turns to stagnation. Stagnation is the enemy of progress and is quite different than rest. God has given us His Holy Spirit in order to avoid one and embrace the other.

A purpose of the Holy Spirit is to foster sanctification in the believer, both individually and corporately. Sanctification is the Christ follower's progress in heart, soul, mind and strength toward a higher level of holiness. Setting the example on day seven of creation, God wove rest into our daily lives; however, one's mind and drive is still toward a closer walk with God, even while at rest. Stagnation is when the drive toward walking with God shifts into park and can happen for an individual and for the church.

God calls pastors to equip the saints to resist stagnation so that a higher level of holiness is always being pursued and our grace-given task of being ministers of reconciliation is always before us. But as skilled as we might be, or *think* we might be, the responsibility of moving people toward that end cannot rest solely upon pastors. We must include many others in this journey, regardless of any personal preference to work alone. Refusing to include others is a sure sign of pride and will soon lead a leader to disgrace (Proverbs 11:2).

Hebrews 10 is known for its lettuce.[9] These five "let us" statements confirm that clearly the clear majority of following Jesus is to be done together; therefore, biblical application environments need to be set up for this to happen. I have made it my personal commitment to supply contextual resources (avenues to apply) for biblical expectations that I teach. While simultaneously encouraging personal creativity and responsibility, I try to give a menu of tools that will assist our church in living out what God expects instead of only teaching for knowledge and expecting them to find their way on their own.

---

[9]There are five lettuce ("let us") statements the author encourages Christ followers to embrace. When I came to this passage while teaching through Hebrews, I took five heads of lettuce and tossed them out to our church as we examined what it biblically means to "let us spur one another", "let us not give up meeting together", and so on. Some have expressed concern if I feel led to use watermelons at some point.

There is such a thing as "potty parity". Perhaps you don't know of such law on the books in your state, but there is such a law in Florida.[10] Potty parity is a guideline for the number of "potties" that are to exist in a bathroom in correlation to gender. In general, there are to be more potties available for women than for men. We discovered this rule when overhauling our church bathrooms. After explaining this rule, the architects developed concept design options for our leadership team to consider. I learned the initial concept design would then be followed by engineering drawings followed by plumber drawings, electrical drawings, and toilet paper drawings (just kidding). But before we could have the contractor begin the remodel, a drawing framework needed to be in place. Without them, workers would not be working toward a unified goal. As a pre-determined direction is essential for the remodeling of bathrooms, it is exponentially more important for the health of the church.

In the early days of my pastorate, our leadership team began a series of discussions about the direction our church needed to take. Both church and community struggles were laid on the table. A glaring issue was confusion about the purpose of the church. With a record number of churches scattered throughout our county, each with different theology on Christian belief and practice, we were hearing some in our community were uncertain about what a biblical

---

[10]If you are looking for some reading material, may I recommend this article
https://en.wikipedia.org/wiki/Potty_parity

Christian truly was.[11] Additionally, because of some struggles in Ferris Hill's past, our people shared the same uncertainty. Toward this end, we embraced our overarching purpose to be "developing authentic followers of Jesus Christ." Each word holding volumes of explanation:

- Developing- people with no relationship with Jesus and those who do but need to grow in holiness;
- Authentic- not fake, identical in public as in private;
- Followers- moving people beyond belief and agreement to application of God's word;
- Of Jesus Christ- we are always clear that we are rooted in the One and Only.

But how would we frame this out?

We reduced our purpose to three different "drawings." Worship, Sharing (Evangelism), Serving (Ministry). To give some memorable handles, we uniformed the language to Reaching Up, Reaching Out, and Reaching In. We realize this is not unique or original, but it is very helpful and meaningful for us. I'll never forget the times with staff at a table in my office hashing out the order: "does worship need to precede our ministry?" "Should we have our

---

[11] I'll never forget talking to a new believer at the gym who had given up on church altogether because the differences in beliefs between the many churches in our area so confused her. The next few months was a mix between answering her questions and working out.

evangelism drive our worship?" Dozens more questions were wrestled with. Ultimately, we settled that our Worship (ReachUP) - loving the Lord with all our heart, soul, mind and strength – would naturally fuel us to Share (ReachOUT) – go into all the world and make disciples – would naturally fuel our desire to do this together and Serve (ReachIN) – spurring one another on toward love and good deeds. Could another church flip these statements around and it work? Definitely. But this was the blueprint for us.

We took these three statements, that we began to refer to as "the R3 journey", and placed them everywhere: newsletter, website, invite cards, and even organized our worship guide around this framework. From that point on, every ministry option that came before us was filtered into this framework. If it fit, without forcing it, we proceeded. If not, we declined. But how could we keep our people from becoming stuck in one area and, instead, move our people along the R3 journey?

I'm a Jeep owner. It's been a long-time joy of mine to travel our area without doors, windows or roof. When becoming a Jeep owner, I noticed there is a community of Jeep lovers who look out for each other. There's even a wave. My son and I went to a Jeep show at a store near our home. Jeeps were lifted and retro-fitted with seemingly endless add-ons. On most of these Jeeps I noticed that they all had winches attached to their front bumper. It seemed they were *expecting* to get stuck or in the least expecting *someone else* to get stuck. (I didn't buy a winch that day, but I did get their contact information.) Jeep owners value movement. Rough terrain or muddy paths should never be a reason to stay stuck where you are. As Christ followers navigating the path God has blazed before us and invites us to follow, we need to be prepared as well.

Developing authentic followers of Jesus also requires a value of movement. Some Christians have a natural draw towards worship and prayer, reaching UP, but tend to shy away from sharing their faith, reaching OUT, or are hesitant to take their needed place within the body of Christ, reaching IN. A healthy church has ministry mechanisms, catalysts, which foster movement to reduce Christ followers from getting stuck. To move our church toward a higher level of holiness and our preferred future, we needed to introduce "winches" into the church to move, sometimes pull, people along the R3 journey. We needed to do this together, within community, spurring one another on toward love and good deeds. We implemented three ministry catalysts to help with movement: 1) Sunday School; 2) Battle Buddies; 3) and Prayer ministry.

Sunday School

God designed the Christian life to be lived out in community. Dozens of times the Bible describes the Christian life with "each other" terminology (ex. forgive each other, pray for each other). Sadly, an American individualistic attitude has prevented followers of Jesus from achieving their redemptive potential. An old Chinese proverb holds, "While you might go faster by yourself, you will go further with others." One of our catalysts, winches, of "other" living is our Sunday School ministry.

(For clarification, I did not introduce Sunday School to our church. This ministry was there at day one while Ferris Hill was still a mission church in the late 1940's. However, I did introduce a redirection this ministry needed to help us get unstuck and head for our preferred future.)

There are endless names to describe the small group ministry in today's churches: Connect Groups, Life Groups, Bible Study Fellowships and probably a few dozen more.[12] Whatever the label you might have in your church, I am referring to the small sub-gatherings of members and guests, Christians and seekers, who come together for Bible Study and sharing life outside of the corporate worship gathering of the entire church. We call ours Sunday School, and we place high value on this ministry.

I attend a class each week. Over the years I have also taught classes when needed (2nd grade, 4th - 5th grade, and Young Adults). I have taught for two reasons: one, need; two, more need. One, I taught because there was unavoidable need in a particular age, and a new class had to be formed. I will quickly admit that teaching children is outside of my comfort zone.

---

[12] A good article on the meaning on naming a small group can be found at
http://www.lifeway.com/groupministry/2014/09/09/call-it-sunday-school-or-another-name-does-it-matter/

While I do not routinely scare children, I am not the Pied Piper who joyously leads them like my father.[13]

As our transportation ministry continued to bring in more kids, the ministry need grew differently than the other age areas and the ministry structure needed to grow as well. We needed another class to properly disciple, sometimes coral, the children God blessed us with. Further, I never want to communicate that any ministry area is beneath me as the pastor. Teaching in areas that were known to be outside my comfort zone gave the example that everyone needed to be willing to roll up their sleeves and serve for the sake of the mission. Secondly, I taught in order to prepare the way for someone to take it over once they were discipled and trained.

Our church has seen most of its growth from people who have had little or no background in church. While that excites us, it also creates some *good* problems. Though more people are engaging in Sunday School, about 80% of worship attenders, and realizing that revitalization is expedited when adding new units, we were limited on who we could move into a teaching role. Some adults were just being introduced to Noah and his big boat while others thought the Lord's Supper was a covered dish luncheon (this actually happened.[14]) And so I taught

---

[13] I have seen pictures and heard numerous testimonies of the magnetic personality my father has upon children when he serves on international mission trips. I am very proud of him.
[14] I told Raymond, a 30 year old new Christian, the week of his baptism that we were going to observe the Lord's Supper the next Sunday. Excited to participate, he brought a bag of dinner rolls

where needed, and still do.

We desire for Sunday School to be a place where Biblical principles become tangible – where the theological rubber meets the practical road. To foster application, our class leaders are asked to set up their class structure and class time according to our R3 journey. Each class has someone(s) focused on reachUp, usually the teacher along with a prayer coordinator. Another person or persons who focus on reachOUT- this is the outreach person(s) of the class who ensures follow-up and assimilation with church guests and who encourages the class to brainstorm who they could invite from their network of relationships, and then plan ministry opportunities to engage in a mission project a couple of times a year. Another person(s) is in charge of reachIN. These members are charged with overseeing the care relationships of the class, coordinating fellowships as well as informing the class of service opportunities within the church. Our leaders are asked to give weekly class time to each area- though the time does not have to be equal. Through keeping each area before the group, everyone is reminded of the value of moving along the R3 journey – worshipping, sharing, and serving.

At our monthly small group leader training, the third Sunday afternoon of the month at four, we evaluate how we are doing so that we can monitor and grow together in the unified direction we all agreed on.

---

the next Sunday. He thought the Lord's Supper was dinner on the grounds.

I have been encouraged to see people who are seemingly disconnected in the corporate worship gathering begin to invite their friends or find a place of ministry because of personal encouragement they received in Sunday School.

Angela was in one of our co-ed classes. In her late 40's, she had overcome a rough past and we were blessed to have a front row seat to her life transformation. In 2015 she felt called to serve on our Haiti mission team. Since this was her first trip, extra vaccines were needed totaling over $100, causing a major burden for her. Unbeknownst to her, her Sunday School class collected money for her vaccines and surprised her one Sunday morning. That one gesture of love caused a rippling effect of service within that class that extended down to the people of Haiti. This was another reminder that Sunday School is the place where you will feel most cared for and loved.

Because we feel so strongly about the power of Sunday School we tell prospective church members, "if you want people to check-in on you in the good times and bad, if you want to be on the receiving end of personal ministry, then get in a Sunday School class. We have no "plan B." But what about when the hard moments come in life? When "unspoken" is all that is written in the class prayer book? That's why we have battleBUDDY.

battleBUDDY

Our small city is in the panhandle of Florida, next

door to Pensacola, a hub of military bases. I can get to five different military installations within a one hour drive (NAS Pensacola, NAS Corey Station, NAS Whiting Field, Hurlburt Field – Air Force, and Eglin Air Force Base). If you are a pilot in the Navy, Marines or Coast Guard, there is a very high chance you will spend some time in our mission field. Consequently, we are blessed to have a high number of veterans in the panhandle who return to live in our area after serving our country.

Kevin is one of the veterans in our church. During the time I was prayerfully researching a needed discipleship model for our church, a breakfast meeting with Kevin took an unexpected direction. What happened in this conversation is what I call a "holy collision." Kevin was recalling his early days in boot camp some thirty years earlier. Upon stepping off the recruiter's bus, he was immediately assigned someone who he was responsible for looking after and also who was also responsible for looking after him- his battle buddy. Kevin said, "You and your battle buddy shared a bunk, ate together, double-checked each other's gear, and made sure you got to where you needed to be on time...and got out. If your battle buddy failed, you failed. If you didn't have the needed gear on your person, your commander would look to both you and your battle buddy. The commanding officer held both responsible." (Do you see where this is going?)

For me, what Kevin was describing was the picture of the church. As Christians, we have numerous "each other(s)" that we are to participate in;

that God, our Eternal Commander-In-Chief, expects of His followers. And in reflection of the perfect community that exists within the Trinity, the bride of Christ, the church, is to enjoy biblical community as well as accomplish the work He has given us to do. Ecclesiastes 4:10 says, "Pity the man who has no one to pick him up." We realize that while everyone needs a small group to be there for you – like Jesus had the twelve disciples, a closer and more intimate group also has its place – like Jesus had Peter, James and John. We need a personal winch.

Since our church already embraced the military culture, if not personally they had patriotically, we developed the battleBUDDY discipleship model. Everyone in our church, especially those in Sunday School classes, is expected and encouraged to have a battleBUDDY. We want to ensure that someone has got your back. We want to ensure you have the contact information of someone who can help you get unstuck.

We realize that there is a higher level of vulnerability when a person moves from hiding in the rows of the corporate worship gathering to sitting in a circle within a Sunday School class. Discussions are more personal. Life is shared. Struggles are vocalized. And this is a good thing. But we know hesitancy remains for the most vulnerable parts of life to be vocalized in a small group setting. Group closeness varies as it is an open group for anyone to come in at any time – plus you only have one hour a week.

BattleBUDDY is positioned so that you have someone to love you through the "unspoken" circumstances each of us go through and to have someone who will put our feet to the holy fire when spiritual stagnation wants to move in. We encourage groups of two but sometimes they morph to include more. A few of our guys have gathered to form what they have termed "battle buddy battalions." Oorah!

At battleBUDDY sign-up, you and your "buddy" receive a packet with a *battleBUDDY Bio* form to complete and exchange, a list of questions to guide your meetings, plus a couple of other helpful resources. Whenever you meet with your battleBUDDY, usually weekly or bi-weekly, the two work through the accountability questions (see Appendix 1.) This creates the accountability needed to move a person along the R3 journey and deal with life issues that can become road blocks.

All battleBUDDY conversations are confidential. We just ask our Sunday School teachers to keep a log of the battleBUDDYies in their class so they can encourage "buddies" from time to time. We also have a male and female coordinator to help connect new "buddies" and recommend resources with requested needs.

We realize that our Sunday School classes can't deal with all issues that people faces; battleBUDDY helps customize and personalize spiritual growth. We have also supplied suggested resources on our website if more assistance is needed on an issue. In addition to asking each other the hard accountability questions, a major part of battleBUDDY time is prayer. Prayer is the primary catalyst, our nuclear fuel, for life on the R3 Journey.

Prayer

Though music is a vital part of the church, Jesus did not call His church a house of music; though Bible study is a crucial part of the church, Jesus did not call His church a house of Bible study. Jesus instructed, "My house shall be called a house of prayer for all nations." (Matthew 21:13; Isaiah 56:7). He reinforced the Father's priority for relationship with His people like He had pre-Fall with Adam, journeying with Moses, and how Isaiah prophetically penned. However creative, strategic, or relevant that we might strive for our church to be, we cannot stray from the priority of prayer if we are to see revitalization come into our church and spread into our community and on to the nations. A prayerless church is destined to run out of energy.

I have a confession; I take *5-hour Energy*. A couple of times a week I take thi s little B12 boost of energy goodness to make it through a long afternoon – especially if I greeted the morning unusually early. But sooner or later the micro-boost runs out leaving the health of my body untouched. Similarly, while our new ministry endeavors and creativity might give microbursts to our church, the freshness will soon fade and the health of your church body will be left untouched. Prayer penetrates to the core of the church body to bring true revitalization.

E.M. Bounds wrote, "The Church is looking for better machinery; God is looking for better men."[15] As we sought to position our church for sustained internal health and external impact, I ashamedly admit that prayer wasn't as high a priority as it should have been. We were focused on the better methods. As a result, we only got the results our earthly resources could muster. Additionally, weariness quickly began to move in and receive mail. Consequently, the fruit of our labors were little. Our endless pursuit to make the Bible come alive drove us to see prayer not as a side endeavor to our work, but rather the actual work.

I enjoy developing strategies, policies and guidelines to strengthen organizations in the community and especially within God's house. (I confess I'm an admin nerd). But without prayer, even the best of strategies can seem like you are trying to run a marathon in a straight-jacket. Prayer frees you. Prayer supplies the clarity where there was confusion and the strength where there was struggle. While I am thankful for the culture of prayer in our church, we have a long way to go to be the people of prayer and house of prayer that God desires.

Some of our folks are comfortable serving monthly on our prayer team, both in service and in the

---

[15] Bounds, E.M., *E.M. Bounds on Prayer, Book 6: Power Through Prayer,* (Whitaker House Publishing, 1997), p. 468.

prayer room, while others have only mastered the art of *submitting* prayer requests. One of the greatest tools we have seen to mature our prayer life is seeing answered prayers. On the back wall of our worship center is a 4'x8' board with the label, "God Answers Prayer." We used an online printing company to make us a red stamp that reads "Prayer Answered." Each week we ask for updates to submitted prayer requests. As we become aware of the answers, we stamp them and hang them up. Periodically, we take time during our Sunday morning service to call up people who have seen prayer answered so they can have the privilege of stamping their card and hanging it up.

Seeing all the "prayer answered" cards has reminded our people of the power of prayer, so more people are praying. Further, there is a greater expectancy of prayer as I have often heard remarks, "Pastor, I am lifting up my neighbor for salvation. I can't wait to stamp my card and see their name on the board." I have also observed that answered prayer is a powerful tool for ministry recruitment. As people gaze at the back wall filled with "prayer answered" they want to get in on what God is doing. Therefore, when a ministry opportunity arises, we make it a matter of prayer.

Being and Doing

Sunday School, battleBUDDY and prayer are not designed to get people busy doing more activity. While these catalysts do serve the purpose of moving our people to put ministry plans into practice, the bigger goal is moving them into a higher level of holiness – which often cannot be put on a calendar. Jesus said that keeping His commands is evidence of our love for, and friendship with, Him (John 14:15, 15:14). Our desire is to give the people of Ferris Hill tangible and practical ways to keep those commands. Further, since there is the "lettuce" statements, we wanted to also keep them together so that when life is over we can confidently declare like Christ Jesus did, "I have finished the work you have given me to do" (John 17:4).

To Consider
1. In 10 words or less, what am I hoping to accomplish through my pastorate at this church?
2. What 3-5 understandable steps are needed to get us there?
3. In order to prevent stagnation, what could we put in place to keep people moving?
4. How could I get our people to remember our process?
5. Who would be the 3-5 people that need to help me answer questions 1-4?
6. When is the best time of year to get together to work on this? (For instance: not between Thanksgiving and New Year's)
7. Alternate: What have I been trying to do that our people would say is confusing or unclear?

CHAPTER 4
REAL RELIGION

When I was in high school, our family took a road trip to visit relatives who took us to a local buffet. When my dad saw the price, he gave me strict instructions to fill up. I, not wanting to be a disobedient son, enjoyed the buffet to the point I was waddling as we headed back (yes, I did engage in gluttony at this family occasion). What makes buffets so enjoyable is that you only put on your plate the culinary delights which you most enjoy while unashamedly passing over the less desirable dishes (I don't think I have ever put carrots on my plate at a buffet).

This buffet mentality is often applied to the Bible. We pick and choose which teachings we enjoy and fill up on them (ex. welcoming children, asking anything in prayer, seeking blessings of God that are exceeding and abundant); while skipping over the less desirable passages. However, one's faith comes alive through the contextual application of *all* Scripture (James 1:21; John 15:14; 1 John 2:3-6).

When my systematic study through the Bible came to Matthew 25:31-46, I could not pass it by when seeking to serve spiritual nutrition to our church. Here's the crux:

> *"Then He will answer them, 'Truly I say to you, to the extent that you did not do it [supply food, water, shelter, clothing] to one of the least of these, you did not*

do it to Me.'" (Matthew 25:45)

Just when I thought I could have my own *pass-over*, the dish of James 1:27 presented pure and undefiled religion.

> *"Pure and undefiled religion in the sight of our God and Father is this: to visit orphans and widows in their distress, and to keep oneself unstained by the world." (James 1:27)*

Ultimately, it was the message of Isaiah 58 that was a super-sized dish I could not skip. Soon this chapter became a main dish of our church no matter how undesirable it seemed to be from time-to- time. In this chapter, the prophet Isaiah is raking God's people over the coals. Sadly, their worship was little more than ritual. They went through the motions hoping that by checking off all the boxes (e.g. standing with the right posture on the right day) that God would look upon them with favor.[16] God was not impressed. Once again, like a parent to a stubborn child, God outlined authentic worship.

> *"Is it a fast like this which I choose, a day for a man to humble himself?*
> *Is it for bowing one's head like a reed*
> *And for spreading out sackcloth and ashes as a bed?*
> *Will you call this a fast, even an acceptable day to the Lord?*

---

[16]Their "check the box" mentality reminds me of the offering envelopes I had as a kid where we would check the box for completed spiritual tasks during the past week, such as Bible brought and contacts made. Remember those?

> *⁶ "Is this not the fast which I choose,*
> *To loosen the bonds of wickedness,*
> *To undo the bands of the yoke,*
> *And to let the oppressed go free*
> *And break every yoke?*
> *⁷ "Is it not to divide your bread with the hungry*
> *And bring the homeless poor into the house;*
> *When you see the naked, to cover him;*
> *And not to hide yourself from your own flesh?"*
> *(Isaiah 58: 5-7)*

With these passages now piercing my heart and mind, I returned to my guiding question – What would Jesus do if He were the pastor? After two seconds of thought, I knew the answer: Apply it. But how? I brought these passages before our church asking some really difficult questions: What do you think God expects us to do with these passages? What would the application look like in your life individually, in our church life corporately and in the surrounding community? Though difficult, would we want God to evaluate our church by saying, "Well done" or "What were you thinking?"

In forging the path that the Holy Spirit was prompting us to blaze, I recalled those initial home interviews and some of the stories shared with me of local service projects they had done decades earlier. With this burden to honor God, contextually apply all His word, and under-shepherd the sheep of Ferris Hill I had attempted to lead for six months, we began the "I-58 Benevolence Ministry" (based on Isaiah 58).

My wife will tell you that onions are not one of my favorite foods. If we get a pizza with onions on it, she mercifully takes my onions and gives me her bacon- the modern man's manna. Onions are deceiving. There is always much more there than what you first see. There is an abundance of layers.

We found *I-58* to be an onion ministry. The clothing needs of the community soon revealed the food needs of the community which soon revealed the financial needs of the community that soon revealed a waterfall of other needs (i.e. education, joblessness, transportation, medical, and more). We quickly realized that we could not do everything. Nor should we. But there were other churches and organizations in the community, thankfully, who were doing a great job in a certain area, and we guided people with their requests accordingly.

If you have ever seen the Christmas movie *Miracle on 34th Street* you will recall that the Clause strategy was to direct people to Gimbels Department Store if Macy's didn't have the requested product. This marketing style of deferring to the competition was viewed as industry-shattering customer service. In our benevolence ministry, we try to take a similar approach. While we might not have a certain ministry resource, we want to be meaningful partners with the community and sister churches so that we can best direct and serve those who come in our doors, not just saying, "sorry." We happily direct those requesting needs to other churches and agencies for further assistance, and we keep an updated list of area resources, with times and contact numbers, in a bin outside our office for inquirers to pick up anytime. This ministry strategy has fostered great partnership between our churches and community organizations. We don't embrace turfism. We are happy to spread the resources around and work together for the betterment of the community. It is because of this high level of partnership that our county, Santa Rosa, became the first Nationally Certified Safe Community. One of the evaluators mentioned that the involvement of the churches in the community was a key component they wanted to share around the country (more on that in chapter 7). I am proud to be a resident here and for our church to play a small part in the county getting that distinction.

I enjoy pastoring, planning and leading "in a fitting and orderly way" (1 Cor. 14:40). But God seems to enjoy teaching me flexibility as a recurring life lesson. There are many times where I have struggled between the fitting and the flexible.

Before we began to promote to the community that we were beginning a food and clothing ministry, people from the surrounding area began to drop off donations. Again, we had *not* publicized our "plans." Flexibility lesson moment. Further, we did not yet have shelving in place to hang any clothes. Flexibility lesson part two. (On a side note: once we did install shelving, we continually modified them for the first year to support the weight as I got tired of walking in the room to see everything had fallen. Again, flexibility.)[17] We converted the choir room into I-58 headquarters since all music activities were taking place in the worship center. *Fitting* flexibility.

Some of our ministry trajectory came in response to the needs revealed on the free demographics report I received from NAMB and the Florida Baptist Convention my first week. But we weren't serving numbers, we were striving to reach people. One of the blessings of I-58 is meeting the community. While we have other ministries where we leave the campus to enter the "mission field", I-58 is a ministry where the community comes to the campus. There are several people who stop by when our food and clothing ministry is open because they needed a friend, not because they needed a resource. Eugene was one such relationship.

Eugene stopped by our benevolence ministry in early 2007. He kept returning to get odds and ends but finally said he just needed the conversation. A veteran with unreliable family relationships, Eugene needed someone with whom he could sort out life. Over the years it has not always been easy to love Eugene (more like hugging a porcupine with dynamite strapped to his back). Threats, legal counsel and various levels of uneasiness has described our relationship. But he has taught us a lot about ourselves – how God must view us when we act unloving, what it means to turn the other cheek when

---

[17] For those with clothes ministries who use wire shelving, I STRONGLY encourage you to get the metal brackets that attach to the wall on top and bottom. It will save you much heartache.

the easier option is payback, walking the second mile when it would be much easier to walk away, and how to be a servant. For instance, I helped Eugene move into a new apartment just a couple of months after he had threatened me with physical harm and mentioned that he had plans to plant illegal drugs in staff vehicles. Like I said, not always easy to love. I contend this is why the "least of these" ministries were so important to Jesus and stressed so strongly to those who would follow Him (Matthew 25:40).

If we truly invest in applying Isaiah 58, James 1, 1 John 2 and the like, we will quickly gain, not just a different view point on our own community, but a clearer view of ourselves and a greater appreciation for the grandeur of God's grace. Sure, it would be easier to *avoid* serving what society may deem "the least of these." It would also be less stressful, with less headaches, less mess, less risk, less unappealing smells, less financial investment, and less a lot of junk. I can only guess that a "less" rationale passed through God's mind when He was laying out the plan of extending grace to secure our redemption – the first benevolent strategy.

Over time, *I-58* helped to change how the community viewed our church. It helped to rebuild trust in the community formed from struggles in our past. Those troubled stories of the past faded, and our benevolent character opened the doors for future opportunities. One such opportunity is our Cold Weather Shelter.

Until the winter of 2007, the only option for the homeless or heatless in our county was to commit a crime so they could warm up in jail, or to travel twenty miles to Pensacola where there were more resources. Our county had no shelters for the homeless when the temperature dropped. Sadly, many committed petty crimes just to get warm. To address this community need, we partnered with the local police to be a place where they could bring those they found with no other place to go. That first year, officers dropped off a couple of people who were being released from jail but with no housing options for the night and one other person who begged them to take them to jail, without committing a crime, just to get warm.

We learned a lot of lessons that first year. Our coordinator and her family spent many nights in the Fellowship Hall with guests. Each of us took our frequent turns since we didn't yet have all the volunteers we needed to be fully staffed. Needless to say, none of our formal education or ministry backgrounds prepared us to lead a church *and* a shelter. (I have thought often of teaching a seminary class on "what I wasn't taught in seminary but wish I had.")

We are never satisfied with how we are doing ministry. Forever evaluating what and how we are doing, learning lessons along the way, we have continually adjusted our strategy to make it easier on our volunteers, and to address the deeper needs of our guests.[18]

By the next year, 2008, we became a little better organized and partnered with the county's Emergency Operations Center (EOC) to be the Cold Weather Shelter (CWS) for the county. From December till March, when the temperature drops below 40 degrees, we open our Fellowship Hall for the homeless and heatless. Currently, we have seven teams of five. Two people who serve as check-in, two who stay overnight; and at least one person who provides a home cooked meal. Each team is on-call one night a week. If the temperature is projected to drop below 40 degrees, we activate the team, call the EOC who notifies the media, place "CWS open" signs in visible areas in the community, and change our marquee to "open."

While our CWS serves a great physical need, it has also given us the opportunity to share the gospel with people our path doesn't routinely cross. Over the years we have had the privilege to see several guests (we always seek to roll out the welcome mat to everyone, regardless of background, who come on our campus– they are more than visitors) come to faith in Christ where we then baptize them. To this day they remain to be valuable members of our church family.

---

[18] Continual evaluation is something we highly value. There is never a time where we lay a ministry aside and call it perfect or permanent. We are forever tweaking as we learn and grow. This "never-ending tweak" mentality has kept us ministry limber and not ministry rigid. Methods change, the message doesn't.

We still recall with great excitement the day when we baptized seven of our guests!

Our desire is for all of our CWS guests to gain reliable housing. Because of the generosity of our church, community, and partnerships with the local organizations, we have been able to see several dozen guests gain housing, either in our area or by getting them back home with family in another part of the state or country – that makes us happy. And when they leave knowing they have an eternal home in heaven, we become ecstatic.

Our guests come in all shapes and sizes – families with children, single men, single women, transients, elderly women, those only with a car, those with a cherished bicycle. One woman felt she was the *Rose of Sharon* in a previous life while another guest claimed to be engaged to a local female police officer who kept stopping him just so she could flirt. Some guests leave the CWS placing much joy in our hearts and others give us grief and frustration (probably like God has toward us). If our I-58 team compiled all of our life stories, it would be a book in itself. But one chapter would include Tommy.

Tommy was a young man in his late twenties who was addicted to alcohol. While he came in sober to the shelter, he spent his days consuming all the alcohol that he could. I often took him to get side jobs or day labor but soon learned those resources only supported his unhealthy habits. One evening before our Wednesday service, I offered to take

Tommy to rehab the following day. He was floored by our generosity. To celebrate entering rehab the next day, and knowing he could not come into the shelter drunk, he spent the cold night in the woods drinking one more time till he passed out. He showed up a couple of days later but was *not* wanting to go to rehab. When he was sober, I shared the gospel repeatedly with him. He thanked me but expressed he was "twenty-seven and had plenty of time to get right with God." The shelter closed for the season a few days later. Fast forward one month, we received word that Tommy's body had been found on the beach washed up behind a local business. I still hear his voice telling me, "Pastor, I am young; I have plenty of time to get right with God." He didn't. He wasn't guaranteed tomorrow. None of us are. The urgency of sharing the gospel increased for me and for our church.

As we walk alongside those who come through the *I-58* ministry door, other unexpected ministries surface as some of our guests struggle with making right decisions. That means they can live on the brink of what is and is not legal. Consequently, I have spent many hours holding counseling sessions in the interview room of the local jail, I have testified before judges having had a front row seat to people who had a recent history of unwise decisions. I know several Department of Children and Family workers by first name and even have become friends with some of the workers affording us the privilege of being an assistance to *them* where we can speak into families' life from a biblical perspective. We have a dedicated computer in our office, donated by DCF, for families to apply for any assistance or build resumes and develop budgets. We permit the homeless to use our church address to receive their mail. Our collective heartbeat has morphed into a relentless pursuit by many of our families, originally quite hesitant, to individually apply Isaiah 58 and other similar passages.

Our chairman of deacons, Bryan, is a guy who is a jack-of-all-trades type of servant but wasn't known for children's ministry or spending inordinate amount of time with those in poverty. His wife Barbara, yes; him, no. But it has been a thrill to see his family now serving as a foster family, even adopting their first foster child and renovating a home near our church campus into a transition home to help people out of homelessness. Another example is the Bryant's, taking in two children and serving as their guardians for more than three years and counting. Or Christina, overcoming a difficult domestic history, finally landing a job at a fast-food restaurant where she regularly buys meals for the homeless and helps others get a job. Or the Stephens, pursuing to adopt a teenager in Haiti. Or Barbara, becoming a payee for a single man who is mentally handicapped. Or Tom, overcoming a pornography addiction during his unchurched years but now coordinating our CWS. And I could go on.

I am often asked of the financial burden the "least of these" ministries places upon our church. Truthfully, very little. We regularly receive donations across our community and across the country from people thanking us for what we do and wanting to partner in a ministry they don't have in their own church.   While our church has been extremely generous, both financially and with their time, the I-58 ministry has reaffirmed to me that you cannot out give God when you are partnering with Him in what He has outlined for us to do in His word.   Let me illustrate our heart through this classic story:

> *A mother, wishing to encourage her son's progress at the piano, bought tickets for a Paderewski performance. They found their seats near the front of the concert hall. The mother found a friend to talk to and the boy slipped away. When eight o'clock arrived, the spotlights came on, and only then did they notice the boy on the piano bench innocently picking out "Twinkle, Twinkle Little Star." The master appeared on the stage and quickly moved to the keyboard. "Don't quit—keep playing," he whispered to the boy. Leaning over, Paderewski reached down with his left hand and began filling in a bass part. Soon his right arm reached around the other side, encircling the child, to add a running obbligato. Together, the old master and the young novice held the crowd mesmerized. In our lives, unpolished though we may be, it is the master who surrounds us and whispers in our ear, "Don't quit— keep playing." And as we do, he augments and supplements until a work of amazing beauty is created.*

This is how we feel about partnering with God.   We have come with some basic willingness to pluck out "real religion" upon the strings of ministry.   Looking at our efforts, it doesn't look like much.   But God has been faithful to come around us and whisper into our willingness, "Don't quit – keep playing" and something way beyond our abilities has taken shape. I have no idea what the context of the community is around your church campus. I don't know the demographics or the need. But I do know that opportunities to apply scripture are all around you. I also know that you can't do it well on your own. But God is not looking for those who can "do it all." He is looking for those willing to pluck away at the tune of "real religion" according to the tune of ministry He has composed. If we do, He will be faithful to turn it into a masterpiece. Just start playing. Don't skip this dish.

To Consider:

1. What are 5 verses that the Bible expresses are core components of God's people, individually and collectively?
2. Where are these verses/passages being practically and regularly expressed through our church?
3. What fears or concerns do I have, or our people have, in living these passages?
4. What heart changes need take place if we are going to be an authentic church as Christ sees us?
5. According to the Bible, based off what we should be doing but are not, what could we begin in the next 6 months (though begin praying and preparing for now)?

CHAPTER 5
NUTS AND BOLTS PART 2

We are continuing to unpack the principles that have guided our uphill journey towards revitalization. We've covered six so far:

#1 – The Bible is the Primary Driver

#2 – Application Surpasses Information

#3 – Know What's Important

#4 – Use the Community to Strengthen The Church

#5- Model What You Expect

#6 – Develop for the Future

Let's Keep Going...

Principle #7 – Identify Landmines and Speed Bumps

Before you arrived as pastor there was a history to your church. Even if you are a church planter, there is a good chance many of your people have some sort of church history. This means people are bringing into your leadership arena the good, the bad and the ugly of their past. There are issues in the past that led to a church split or that broke up friendships or that just plain wounded all involved. The issue might not have been the issue at all – it might have been the timing. These painful issues create landmines that can destroy revitalization or build speed bumps that greatly slow it down. A pastor who is going to lead his church toward revitalization and health must detect, uncover and remove such issues.

Discovering the land mines and speed bumps requires a lot of listening. Regardless of the recommendations of church experts, authors, or any successes you might have in your past, you have never pastored your current church before. It is different. For me, there were some healthy church practices I wanted to bring into Ferris Hill because they worked well at my previous church. But after listening to the church's history, I discerned I needed to wait. Our church membership covenant is one example.

Several years before I arrived, the pastor wanted to add a church membership covenant requirement. To be precise, he wanted to duplicate what another church had done. The issue "hit the fan" and played a part in the church going through a major split. When I arrived, I too felt a church membership covenant would be beneficial; however, I soon discovered the history and knew the issue needed to be tabled. Wounds needed to heal. I did wait, and nine years later we embraced a membership covenant without a hitch, and the covenant serves a great part of our church life today.

Remember, your church has unique struggles with a unique history. Always taking the attitude of "I know better" is one of the fastest ways to stall revitalization. No matter how long you are pastoring, never stop listening. While you might have a clear destination, a good and godly destination, how you choose to get there will make or break you. Give every effort to know where the landmines and speed bumps are located.

To Consider:

1   Do I know the key struggles the church experienced before my arrival?

2   What am I currently doing that, while a good idea, might need to wait for a better time?

Principle #8 – Move According to the Direction and Speed of Prayer

When Abraham left Ur to head to the would-be Promised Land, he did so in response to God giving direction and "as the Lord had spoken to him" (Gen. 12). Each movement was a response to God's direction, not selfishly moving any direction he felt and hoping God would bless it. But while the destination and direction are valuable, most leaders get hung up in the speed of the journey. We want to arrive now. Ignoring the fact that God is doing a work while on the journey. When we get ahead of God's prompting we end up doing ministry in our own strength and navigating our church into circumstances God preferred we had avoided. King Saul is one of the more glaring examples.

God permitted Saul, due to the selfish nagging of the people, to be the first King of Israel (Saul accepted it reluctantly). For the most part, he was quite victorious in his endeavors. On one occasion he and the army of Israel were waiting for Samuel the priest to arrive in order for the sacrifice to be made before the battle was to commence. Saul got impatient. But he chose to work on his own timetable instead of God's. He got tired of waiting for Samuel the priest to arrive, and so he performed the sacrifice himself. Samuel arrived shortly after. Saul thought activity and movement was more valuable than obedience. He was wrong. Obedience is better than sacrifice (1 Sam. 15:22). Consequently, the kingdom was torn from Saul not long after. Imagine what would have happened if Saul had only waited thirty more minutes. Samuel would have arrived, and Saul would have fought the battle with God on his side.

For those like me who thrive on productivity, there is great temptation to push forward at all costs. When we lead and pastor like this, we are doing so like Saul- pursuing the sacrifice of ministry productivity instead of the joy of godly obedience. If our churches are going to be places that God builds so the "gates of hell won't prevail" against, it is imperative that we slow down, wait on the Lord, and move at the speed of prayer.

Let me give you a few reasons.

- One, to renew our strength. Moving at the speed of prayer will ensure the strength of the Holy Spirit is fueling our every step and not our limited resources.
- Two, to give time for prayer to work in others. While you might be ready to climb a new ministry

mountain, there are others coming behind you who don't yet have the spiritual legs to climb or the vision to see. Prayer strengthens our faith. Leading your church at the speed of prayer will ensure you have other parts of the body of Christ standing with you when you reach whatever summit God has laid before you.

- Three, God is shaping you into His image as you journey and not just getting you to a ministry destination.

While we can greatly desire to mark off another ministry accomplishment, we must ensure our character is moving toward ever-increasing holiness and walking obediently by His truth alone. It is a sad sight to see those who do much "for Jesus" yet look so unlike Him when it's all said and done. Taking the extra time to lead at the speed of prayer will give margin in your life for God to shape a holy character – which in the long run is the true destination – looking like Jesus. To pull this off demands your meetings move forward prayerfully. Delay moving forward until you have the green light from God and He has shown you that your people are ready, even if reluctantly ready. Such waiting might drive you crazy. But you will have to decide if you want God to fight whatever battles lie before you or if you want to go at it alone. Remember, it might just mean waiting only thirty extra minutes.

To Consider:

1. What role does prayer actually play in my leadership?

2. Am I moving at the speed of prayer or just pushing through on my own? Where can I wait?

Principle # 9 – Structure to Strengthen the Family, Including Yours

There is no perfect schedule for your church – either personally or corporately. Depending on your context, the effectiveness of schedule times and day can shift as much as weather predictions. The options for the winning schedule are lengthy, but there are also schedules that position your family to end up on the losing end.

There is a false leadership premise that says, busyness equals godliness; therefore, churches seeking to be healthy should fill up their weekly schedule so that practically all 168 hours are accounted for. We embrace the premise that meetings, events and a buffet of stylized service choices, outings, sports leagues, more meetings and the like should occupy our calendar. And that's just Sunday and Monday. But consider this: Every hour that you are at the church campus is another hour you are not in the mission field *being* the church and often not being with your family. Now I am in no way, shape or form are discouraging essential ministries that need to take place on the church campus. And I am not ignoring that there are certain sacrifices that the families of those in vocational ministry endure. And I am not discouraging hard work. But is it possible that how and what we are doing is undercutting our family? And what if a streamlined approach could be developed so that people are trained, ministries are developed and your family feels valued?

As Andy Stanley wrote in *Choosing to Cheat: When Family and Work Collide*, you will cheat someone somewhere, either your work or family. After reading that book early in marriage, I asked Candace what time it would be helpful for me to be home each weekday. Her reply, 4pm. Since that conversation, 4pm has been my goal. To assist with this commitment, I heavy-load a couple of days – Sundays and Wednesdays. I schedule counseling on Sunday afternoons and Wednesday evenings (pre and post service). We also established a Sunday afternoon training schedule we called *412*-based off of Ephesians 4:12-for each Sunday at 4pm. Therefore, the first Sunday is our church council, second Sunday our ministry teams (committees) meet, the third Sunday we train our Sunday School teachers, and the fourth Sunday our deacons gather. While this model isn't for everyone, I have not been drawn away from my family and community to attend additional weeknight meetings. Additionally, our student ministry has committed itself for students to be home by 8pm on school nights, and our children's ministry has coupled parent training with Vacation Bible School so all members of the family are growing together.

There are dozens, or hundreds, of people in your church who call you "pastor." But there are only a couple who call you "dad" or "husband" or… Aren't they worth the effort to adjust your church schedule so that at the end of your life they are standing alongside you happy that you served in ministry and better because of it? Without wishing their family member did something else. Without having to deal with the side effect of you not taking care of yourself or them.

To Consider:

1. Does our weekly schedule build up my family? What recommendations would my family make to our church schedule?
2. What adjustments could we begin to make to our church schedule that would strengthen our families and give people time to apply God's word?

Principle #10 – Reel In, Then Give Away

Disorganization encourages everyone to scatter. Without a shepherd clarifying the path ahead, all the sheep will pick their own direction. This is often what a church in decline feels and looks like – everyone seeking to go in their own direction. There must be someone to help bring everyone together. The pastor leading his church into revitalization will need to bring much of the ministry very close. This may be perceived as a leader who just wants to be controlling. And to a degree it is. At times, and for a season, that might be what a leader does. But "bringing ministry close" must be coupled with humility and communicating that this is not permanent and not about you.

When a pastor brings ministry close, he will then work with a few others, in a very hands on manner, to help craft the ministry into a healthy format. As the church then becomes familiar with the

71

healthy format, he can then slowly release it out for others to be the primary overseer. Pastors must be intentional about giving away ministry so they are only doing what they only can do.

A veterinarian will often rescue a hurting animal and then bring it to their clinic so they can be close by for medical attention and rehab. Once health returns, the animal is released. Pastors leading their church through revitalization must embrace this same capture, restore and release mindset. Again, our goal is not to permanently and unnecessarily control everything; but, to give people healthy ministries they can oversee (And when it's all done, give credit to the other person – not yourself).

While the catch and release principle is true for revitalizing ministries, the same holds true for shepherding people. Remember, we as church leaders are not merely in the ministry business, we are in the people business. Unhealthy ministries are often a reflection of hurting people. The pastor/ under-shepherd needs to be sensitive to not ignore the needs of the sheep on the journey to better pastures. It will do you no good to spend endless hours reorganizing ministries and strategizing for a healthy future while your people remain hurting, wounded and straggling behind. It is imperative that you set up a system of relationships, such as Sunday School or some other form of nurture, so that you can monitor and engage where your people are. As we do this, we will bring our people in for a higher level of encouragement, seek to restore and equip, and then release them out to fulfill whatever God gifted them to do in the body.

To Consider:

1. What ministries do I need to bring in closer to better position it for future success?

2. What am I doing today that needs to be properly given away to someone else?

Principle #11 – Hold Direction Tight; Hold Timing Loose

Your church will not always change at the speed you desire. Though God might have plans to bring change and revitalization faster than you planned, this is generally not the case. God usually makes the journey much slower because He wants you to learn primarily about Him during the journey. God uses the journey to shape your character into His image during this time and prepare the entire body of faith to arrive safely at the destination. Further, the more people who are involved and the bigger the "thing", the longer the process will take. But the slowness shouldn't alter the direction or your motivation. If we are not careful and resolute, our impatience can cause us to abandon the mission God has called us to engage.

When God gives you clarity about where your church needs to head, be faithful in leading your people in that direction. However, recognize everyone is coming from different starting points of spiritual maturity and ecclesiastical understanding. And while it is not a bad thing to lay out a goal and plan to get there, don't throw up the white flag if you miss the timeline. For instance, if you want to develop your church to be a praying church, does it really matter if it took thirteen months instead of three? Will another six months or a year on a certain item be that big of a deal if it means decades of health for your church – especially if moving at that speed will result in everyone arriving safely at a revitalized port of ministry instead of having a few people fly overboard because you were moving too fast for their ability to hold on? So be committed to the direction, but hold timing loosely.

To Consider:

1   Would our church say we are clear about the direction we are heading?

2   In what areas am I working where I need to loosen up in regard to timing?

The Growing List

These eleven principles, including chapter one, have guided much of our church and my leadership. I am not suggesting that this list is set in stone. We are continually learning, adding, and adjusting. Nonetheless, these eleven nuts and bolts have greatly aided in the revitalization of our church and the pages that follow will show how we brought them to bear in our church life. What would you add?

CHAPTER 6
YOU SHALL BE...

[8] But you will receive power when the Holy Spirit comes on you; and you will be my witnesses in Jerusalem, and in all Judea and Samaria, and to the ends of the earth." –Acts 1:8

In October 2012 a team from our church went on a mission trip to New York City.[19] The primary purpose of this trip was to pray. Partnering with *Foreign Service Fellowship*[20], our team of nine prayer-walked in front of all 195 mission offices of the United Nations. This was our one-week blitz to prayer-walk the world. Our secondary focus was to meet with the United Nations Ambassador from Haiti.

For years our church had faced different challenges serving the people of Haiti. Before I left the meeting with the Ambassador, I asked if there was any need the Ambassador could think of where our church could assist. He did mention one *small* item – moving about 300,000 people, still in a tent city after the 2010 earthquake, into permanent housing. The Ambassador did not create this need, he only communicated it. The job of the Ambassador is to represent and communicate the interests of his

---

[19] Halloween in Manhattan is a story in itself. For starters, I'll never forget sitting next to a person on the subway wearing a horse head "galloping" to some costume party uptown.

[20] Foreign Service Fellowship is a ministry that builds relationships with each of the missions of the United Nations and seeks to be an evangelistic force to each UN Ambassador.

President and his homeland. If he does this faithfully and successfully, he will hear, "well done."

Jesus made it clear to those who follow Him that they are to be microphones of His gospel and ambassadors of His interests (2 Cor. 5:20) – His witnesses. Further, He promised that He will equip these ambassadors with the power of the Holy Spirit to accomplish this witnessing mission (Eph. 4; 1 Cor. 12:7).

Acts 1:8 is one of the more memorized verses in the Bible. I'm not suggesting it is in the John 3:16 echelon, but it is up there – especially more than Leviticus 19:17. (Go ahead and look it up.) Sadly, memorization doesn't always equate to application. A 2012 Lifeway Research poll found that while 75% of Christians knew they were to share their faith - be witnesses- 60% have never told anyone. James 1:22 exposes the great deception of only hearing the biblical information while neglecting the application.

> *[22]But prove yourselves doers of the word, and not merely hearers who delude themselves."*

Imagine a Navy SEAL knowing precisely where each piece of equipment is stored but never putting it on when called upon to push freedom forward. As pastors and church leaders, we have a responsibility to equip our people to fulfill the work of Christ (Eph. 4:12) and then to properly send them out in the same Spirit that God sent Jesus (Jn. 20:21). While the timeline between teaching and sending doesn't have to be long (think of the instant response of the Samaritan woman at the well in John 4), we do need to have both in place.

After spending some intentional listening time with our people, seeking to discern how we were moving toward spiritual maturity, I found that many were hesitant to share their faith because they honestly were not sure what to say even though they heard the biblical principles taught regularly. Their hesitancy prompted me to give multiple points of application to biblical principles.

The temptation is for me to lay out the principle and expect them to run with it on their own to apply it. I taught the *what*, now you figure out the *how*. This didn't happen. Initiative was low. I have come to learn that this kind of forward-thinking is known as abstract thinking and is quite difficult for many. This is opposed to concrete thinking where there is a clearly defined goal and you work your way back to where you currently are. Though at times a challenge, I strive to teach in a concrete way – even though it may cost me extra time and energy.

I don't honestly think there can ever be too many tools employed to teach people how to share the gospel of grace. Periodically during our Sunday worship service, I use the "Welcome Time" to give a three-minute training on how to share your faith. During these micro-training times, I draw the evangelistic tool, write out the key words and even have the congregation practice with those sitting next to them. I follow this Sunday teaching with a low-tech You Tube video sent through email, posted to our Face Book page, or pin to the front of our website; or, if one is available, direct people how to use an app on their smartphone. As long as the biblical essentials are present – sin, grace, faith, repentance – there are endless ways to be a witness. But where to start?

In 2008 we spent some time overhauling the appearance of our facility (more on that in Chapter 8). While we didn't move any walls, we did coat the walls in different colors to give our campus a new look. We wanted to maximize this two-acre ministry tool God had blessed us with and push "refresh" on our facility. The same is true in being a witness. There are different tools we can use to color our evangelism but sometimes we need a fresh and reliable structure to paint upon. Using the four regions of Acts chapter one as a template, we generated a reachOUT (evangelism) strategy that we could visualize- actually walk on and then put our witness to. We call this plan 4theMISSION. 4theMISSION is simply our four different mission fields with each mirroring the Jerusalem, Judea, Samaria, and ends of the earth witness expectation.

MissionFIELD1 – *"...in Jerusalem..."*

Jerusalem was the original hub of Christianity (or rather "the Way"). When Jesus "shall"-ed Acts 1:8 into existence, Jerusalem was where the temple was, the crucifixion and resurrection as well, and the ascension was about to be there in a few moments. In ten days the Holy Spirit would make His indwelling entrance here. Jerusalem was the city everyone journeyed to for the required collective worship within the Jewish festival system (e.g. Passover, Pentecost, and *Yom Kippur*). Jerusalem was home base.

FHBC views our church campus and the surrounding community as our Jerusalem. Just to be as clear as possible, we acknowledge that the Jerusalem analogy breaks down in various points. We don't view the church campus as the *only* place to meet with God – the torn temple curtain helped to purge that notion. We affirm that each grace-receiving, faith-walking Christ follower is the temple of God (1 Cor. 3:16) as well as being a kingdom of priests (1 Peter 2:9). All that being considered, Jerusalem, in Jesus's day, was the collective meeting place for the people of God. While we go to our individual home bases the majority of the time, our church campus is the sacred gathering place for the church.

Further, just because we travel *to* our Jerusalem doesn't mean that we ignore what *surrounds* Jerusalem, just as Jesus went outside the city wall and encouraged us to do the same (Heb.13:11-14). Taking His cue, we embrace being witnesses both in and around our Jerusalem. This means we are to routinely share the gospel with those who come on our church campus as well as those surrounding it.

Ferris Hill Baptist Church is a hidden church. We are not on a major road and are two blocks away from what locals consider "major." In fact, many who have lived in Milton most of their life have no idea where our church campus is because we are in a section of town where many never venture, even by accident. While this can be discouraging when wanting to be easily seen, we know our location is not an accident. We hold to this even though the demographics of the community have greatly changed in our 65+ years. In addition to giving us our breath, we see that the Bible reveals God is behind even our placement in the world (Acts 19). We cannot waste our location, both individually and collectively. We must redeem it for HIS purpose. This purposed location even carries over to our homes and missionFIELD2.

To establish our missionFIELD1, our Jerusalem, we identified the exact streets that would be our boarders. We expressed that these were not permanent lines we were drawing but only a prayer-arrived starting point that we desired to expand over time. We Google-mapped our area and then drew lines as to what will be *our* Jerusalem. From Ferris Hill Street (on the East) to Byrom Street (on the West) to Munson Highway (on the South) to Magnolia Street (on the North) was our Jerusalem (See Appendix 2). Further, we agreed that whether we lived inside these borders or not, this is *our* Jerusalem. Inside these borders is the place where our church gathered, and this community will be the place where we partner together as collective ambassadors. We will be the witnesses for this community. But how?

We began to brainstorm questions: How can we pray for this community? What would God have us do in this community? Who lives and works in this community? What are the first and last names of the residents? Where do they work, or are they looking for work? What are the needs of this community? What does it mean to be a pastor, be a Sunday School teacher/class, have a youth, have children, or some other ministry in *this* community? We took our questions to God in prayer and also to the streets.

We purchased thirty cardboard survey boxes which local businesses allowed us to display for one month in order to collect surveys. Additionally, multiple teams of two or three spent a few Sunday afternoons going door to door asking residents for a few moments to help us with a survey to discover needs they perceived in their community and what they thought a church could do to address them. After all the surveys were completed, we brought our entire church back together to review the results. We looked for patterns and then identified what appeared to be the priorities, as well as discerning the gaps. After getting alla of those analytics and observations, though eager to speed to the highways and byways, we were NOT ready to get going.

The reason we hit pause is that we don't feel the church exists to merely meet whatever needs might be listed. While we love our community, we don't take our orders from the community. Our community is not our leader. God is our Leader. But in the manner in which Jesus asked the blind man, "what do you want me to do for you" (Mark 10), we wanted to know the current needs so that when God released us we would have some clarity as to how we could be His hands and feet to address both spiritual and physical needs. In the years that followed, we continued to crisscross our "Jerusalem" going door to door praying for families, sharing the gospel, offering tutoring and resume building, providing transportation to church and doctor's appointments, supplying food/clothing, and other opportunities God brought before us. *Love Thy Neighbor* and the *Bless the City Challenge* are two missionFIELD1 events which really stick out for our church.

Love Thy Neighbor was a food distribution project participated in by 80% of our church. We contacted the county school district to identify district employees who often struggled meeting bills during the summer due to being off in the summer (e.g. bus drivers, custodians and cafeteria workers). We ordered food from the local food bank and spent an entire Saturday sorting and organizing our Fellowship Hall for the church-wide mission project the following afternoon. Recognizing many we were serving also struggled with transportation resources, we delivered all the baskets to their homes giving us one on one time to converse and pray with the family.

The *Bless the City Challenge* was an opportunity to unleash creative ideas of our church family. Each of our Sunday School classes were given ten weeks in the summer to brainstorm a one-thousand-dollar idea to bless our city in the fall. Each idea would be presented to an outside panel of judges. The idea had to have a gospel component, be able to involve our entire church and take place within the city limits. After many years of articulating what it meant to BE the CHURCH, I was excited to see the Christ-like love for our city come to life in practical and fun ways. We ended up delivering 9-volt batteries and praying with families during Fire Prevention week – an idea from our second and third graders. But we couldn't stop there.

missionFIELD2 *"...Judea..."*

Yahweh is sovereign God. Though a mysterious partnership exists between man's free will and God's omniscience and omnipotence, God is in control. God's control is not limited only to the big stuff- like the spin rate of the earth; it extends down to the tiniest of details – like the flight habits of a single sparrow. And, not by accident, somewhere within this big sovereign world is where we live. Even within our small church, the diversity of living conditions is wide. Some live in sub-divisions while others are in subsidized housing. Some are in apartments while others are in a nursing home. Some rent, some own, some crash on a friend's couch. Some people are comfortable with their neighbors, and others find themselves with the police on speed dial. Regardless of the diversity, where we live is where we are, and our God-given command to be His ambassador of reconciliation is resolute. In the midst of joining with others in our Jerusalem, we cannot neglect our Judea. We cannot embrace the mission of our church campus while ignoring the everyday mission of our individual neighborhoods.

Judea was the surrounding region of Jerusalem. It was the area where people lived when they weren't ascending to participate in the required worship of Jerusalem. Farming was in Judea, friends hung out in Judea, fathers practiced their trade in Judea.

Allison and Iain are one of our God-fearing, community-loving, country-serving military families. From the time that Iain began to serve out his orders training Coast Guard helicopter pilots at NAS Whiting Field, this precious family began to connect with and serve their neighbors.

Our family was invited to a Labor Day gathering at their home. At this gathering it was so encouraging to see the neighbors they had been praying for and investing in from their kids' school, other military families and those who lived next door. Allison and Iain viewed their place in life and in their neighborhood as a "for such a time as this" opportunity. They wanted to maximize all circles of relationships and the resource of their home for the glory of God.

We live in a day where it is very easy to be isolated from our neighbors. We can pull in and out of our garages without breathing the outside air as well as conduct family activity within the privacy of our castle-like fences. But our mission field extends beyond our driveway to those whom we work with and go to school with. None of these are an accident; rather, each person is a divinely given relationship that we must redeem for God's glory. If not intentional, especially for those introverted like me, we can go decades and never even learn the names of those who we live, learn and work within feet of.

Here in Florida we have been known to have the occasional hurricane. As a native, I've been through more than my fair share. Though I don't care for the loss of utilities that accompany hurricanes, the aftermath brings its own fair share of excitement. Hurricanes bring the opportunity to partner with neighbors at a much higher level. When Hurricane Ivan came to Pensacola (2004), and then Dennis and Katrina (2005), we all hooked our generators together, got our grills working in unison, and took turns helping clean up one another's yard. It was a blast. I was glad when we continued that community life after the air-conditioning came back on. Those days helped me to see my home as something more than a place to sleep – it is a ministry tool to be stewarded.

To jump start Judea, Acts 1:8, thinking, even before we formally called it missionFIELD2, I conducted an exercise during one evening worship service. I asked someone to name a country. I think Zimbabwe was agreed on. Further, I wanted everyone to imagine that they had just been commissioned as a missionary to this country. I then asked, "If you are to be an effective missionary, what questions do you have that need to be asked and then answered?" Those evening worshipers generated a list that included the need for relationships, prayer, language, knowledge of customs, and Bible access: What is the best way to form relationships? What is the language? What is common dress? What is culturally acceptable and what is not? What access to the Bible do they have? I then erased our example country from the heading and replaced it with "your neighborhood." What is the difference between the home front and a foreign mission field? Isn't one man's home another man's mission field? Why don't we view our homeland, our neighborhoods, through the eyes of a missionary? Why should we wait for some outside missionary sending agency to reach those who live around us when we are already here and Jesus has already sent us (John 20:21)? Their answers, for example, helped us realize we shouldn't expect a certain standard of dress for our members and guests and that a pew Bible written on a seventh-grade reading level was best. (Fortunately, and unlike most international missionaries, we didn't need to go to language school.)

To supply equipping resources for missionFIELD2, and before I really knew some already existed, I took some basic training material a couple of missionary agencies published for reaching unreached people groups and modified them for our local context. We realize that there is no *one way* to reach your neighborhood.

Each family in our church lives in a unique neighborhood – even though our city/county is relatively small. We encourage our people to get to know their neighbors. We encourage Mondays to be "Make a Difference Monday" to impact someone in your missionFIELD2. This extends beyond the home to students and the student in the seat next to them and to the employee toward their co-worker next to them. Periodically we will leave space in our Sunday Worship bulletin, get everyone to draw their neighborhood. We then have them write the family names and then spend time in prayer for them. We further encourage seasonal interaction around Christmas, New Year's, Easter, and the start of Hurricane Season. We found that neighborhood block parties are a great way for our people to invite over their next-door families to intentionally build relationships and give gospel influence. Our goal is to have twelve block parties a year, one event across our church a month. We also ask our Sunday School classes to provide backup support to the host and invite families who are planning to host a party the next month to swing by and observe.

A key part of our missionFIELD2 endeavors is prayer. We always want to move at the speed of prayer. Further, our hearts are more ready to act toward our neighbor if we have first been preparing our hearts by praying for our neighbors. We want to see our prayers answered; therefore, our prayer paves the way to practice. Using digital resources like *pray4everyhome.com* we are able to focus our people on praying for their entire neighborhood. Additionally, we set aside the fifth day of every month to encourage everyone to fast from something and pray for five non-Christian friends. We call this "5 on the 5".

We have a dream that because of the diligent work of our people that one day our mission field one and two will merge together. But what about where people tend to avoid?

MissionFIELD3 *"....in Samaria..."*

Samaria was the section of Palestine most people tried to avoid if at all possible. Known for the "half-breeds", both religiously and ethnically, the people on the outside of Samaria tended not to waste brain cells on those inside Samaria. They didn't even want Samaritan sand to get on their sandals. This is the way the people of Haiti are often viewed.

In November of 2009 I was invited to be on a team of four pastors to go to Haiti and conduct pastor training and revivals. My heart fell in love with this country 600 miles south of my state. My heart broke when a magnitude 7.0 earthquake hit on January 12, 2010. The place I had just stood two months earlier was now a pile of rubble. People I just met had loved ones buried in the debris. Though our church immediately engaged in stateside relief efforts, we felt our work in Haiti was not complete.

I returned with a team eight months later on an Association trip this time bringing a couple more from our church to further train pastors, equip other church leaders and conduct a VBS. We returned the following year to continue our people building efforts with a team of seven – this time all from our church. Haiti had become the place to go for missions.

If you were to sit for long in the Port-au-Prince airport you would see a dozen mission groups at any given time. We wanted to go where we were most needed. I received some guidance from the Florida Baptist Convention that the Nord (North) region was in great need. To be precise, no one was going to go to the north shore to the city of Cap-Haitien – the original capital of Haiti filled with 2.1million people. In 2012 seven members from Ferris Hill made the trek. For a week we formed a deep bond with some of the pastors, ministry leaders and children. Though our plans were forcibly adjusted as Hurricane Sandy skirted the island during our stay, the plans for future ministry in this city were planted.

I had been prayerfully considering how ministry training could continue on a more frequent basis than one week a year. God was stirring within me to begin training Haitian pastors. I broached the idea with the Director of Missions for the Nord region. His face lit up as he told me through the translator they had been praying for such training for over three years. But how would we pull it off?

I like technology. Not the greatest at it, but I do enjoy taking advantage of it. Since my family had not been able to travel with me overseas, I had begun to use Skype to communicate back home. I pondered how Skype could be leveraged as a training tool. Our church purchased a compact projector and had it delivered to Haiti through a friend of mine heading down there. Three months later we began our training the third and fourth Saturday of each month. Though the connection is sometimes sketchy, overall it has been an overwhelming success. I email a listening guide to my translator a couple weeks ahead of time, and he translates it into Haitian Creole. On the given Saturday, my face pops up on a screen (which is actually a sheet) in their lean-to church building. I teach, and Ferdly, my translator, re-teaches. Over the years we have taught several subjects including the entire *Systematic Theology* by Wayne Grudem, as well as an Introduction to the Bible class, plus a long list of others.

It was out of this burden to be effective in Haiti that led us to New York in 2012 to pray and meet the UN Ambassador. This burden also showed us in 2014 we could not do our Haitian ministry as usual. Seeking to reflect biblical examples whenever possible, we didn't book a hotel that year. Instead, we stayed in one of the pastor's home. Besides being able to immerse ourselves even deeper into the Haitian culture, we felt this would be a better steward of our church's money and could open more resources to ministry where there was a true need.

On a side note, our teams have never done fundraisers, and we are not a wealthy congregation. We believe that our *entire* church is on the Haiti mission team even though a handful of us are on the ground. We encourage everyone to give to "missions" as this is the need we, the body united and working together toward a common purpose, all have. Because of this corporate giving effort, no one has been prevented from going because of financial strain, and we have not had to seek resources outside for what God has called *us* to do.

The year 2015 proved to be pivotal. After three years of investing in the pastors in CAP, and with the in-country training being in great demand, being limited to the first fifty to register, a transition began to take place. Instead of taking the lead at a VBS, we trained the leaders and then coached *them* to do it. Instead of me teaching monthly, my translator, who became a pastor, did the teaching of the material I sent down, while I was available to answer any questions. We wanted to shift ministry responsibility to the Haitians. We did not want them to be permanently relying on us. As 2 Timothy 2:2 guides, we wanted to teach people who could teach people. This strategy shift has led to exponential increase in ministry beyond the ability of our small church as we have heard of the new churches they are planting, new ministries they are beginning, and the ecclesiastical health Jesus-exalting climate that is returning to this Voo-doo dominated culture. Our ministry in Haiti, our Samaria, has been a place I never want to avoid. But what about those who are completely unreached?

MissionFIELD4- *"...to the very ends of the earth."*

Missional statisticians say there are approximately 11,000 people groups in the world. Of them, about 4,000 have no access to the gospel. This statistic is overwhelming, the need for the gospel is massive, and accomplishing this overwhelmingly massive task is mind-blowing. But what if our small church could partner with big God to just take care of one of them? After teaching on our need to apply *all* of scripture, the unreached-unengaged people groups of the world became part of our conversation. Not knowing where to begin, or even how to pronounce many of the people group names, our church leaders requested that I select the people group I thought we should embrace.

With the assistance of Corina, one of the twenty-somethings in our church with a white-hot love of the nations, we prayed over the "getting there" web page of the International Mission Board.[21] Very soon we felt drawn to the Han-Chinese of an East Asia country. I presented it to the church who, though initially reluctant due to the location of the people group, got fully on board.

For two years we researched their history and prayed for this people group that we Floridians could not be more different than. Because of security risks, we felt it would be years before we would actually step on their soil. We were wrong. Through a God-ordained opportunity, Corina and I were able to join a group of thirteen from Texas and go into this restricted, "closed", country. After the trip, after seeing God's hand all over this ministry possibility, about twenty people signed up to be on a planning team. What first seemed absurd came closer. We began to see this ministry opportunity through God's unlimited eyes and not our limited ones. While we

---

[21] http://gettingthere.imbresources.org/

have a long way to go before planting a church among this people group, literally getting to the moon might be easier, we are slowly moving forward hoping that one day this people group will be crossed off the list. And though most of our efforts have been in prayer, we have seen the "reached" status shift from "no work" to "progress." Prayer works.

"Jerusalem, Judea, Samaria, to the ends of the earth" - four areas that our church is separated from by thousands of miles, thousands of years, yet right outside our door and right now. God has called us to be His witnesses. As authentic followers of Jesus, people who are to be the hands and feet of our Lord, who are ambassadors of our heavenly homeland and our holy head of state, we cannot lay our head to the pillow satisfied with memorizing this passage but failing to apply it. We have no excuse. We have the Holy Spirit indwelling us and empowering us to accomplish it. "You shall be..." We try. We are...4theMISSION.

To Consider
1. What roads or regions comprise the mission field(s) of our church?
2. How can we personalize the mission fields, both local and abroad, for our people?
3. What outreach have we avoided because it was uncomfortable, included risk or was new?
4. How do our actions and attitudes toward outreach reflect that of Christ Jesus? Where do we need to

most work? Where do I need to set a better example?

CHAPTER 7
THE MINISTRY BUTTERFLY EFFECT

Perhaps you know of the "butterfly effect"- the theoretical link between a butterfly flapping its wings somewhere in South America that begins a chain of ecological events that ultimately creates a hurricane or some major atmospheric effect on the other side of the planet. Maybe it is true, maybe not. Add it to the list of questions asked during orientation on the first day of heaven. (I am really hoping for a Q&A session anyway). Regardless, I cannot deny the chain reaction of endless doors for ministry that I have personally experienced that have contributed to our church's revitalization journey.

When Candace and I moved to Milton, our daughter Baleigh was twenty months old and we soon discovered our son Elijah was on the way as well. We were not thinking about the local schools. We were thinking about overcoming diapers. Before we knew it, Kindergarten was upon us. Though Candace and I both grew up in public school, it was a new phase for us to turn our little girl loose upon this new frontier. Following the example of my parents while my sister and I were in school, I was already planning to volunteer.

My parents were also always helping chaperoning school events. Mom served as the room mom and dad helped load band equipment or set up for special events. I never found it odd or intrusive for them to be there, they just loved my sister and me, and it showed through their servant's heart. Till this day, they tell me of people my sister or I went to school with who come up to them in the community and remember them from serving on a trip or in a classroom. I am fortunate to have some good shoes to emulate.

Since Friday was the day I took off from the office, I set aside Friday mornings to volunteer at Baleigh's school. Each week I checked in with her teacher to see if I could help grade any work, listen to kids read or just be of any help. I also checked in with the administration to see if I could help them in anyway. Soon, I could be found most Fridays filing records and doing odds and end tasks of teachers and administration.

During my second year, Baleigh's first grade year, I was asked to take the helm of the WATCH D.O.G.S. Program – Dads Of Great Students. This is a national program by Fathers.com which strives to get dads on campus to volunteer. It is driven by the proven observation that learning goes up and discipline issues go down when dads are on campus. In this program, we would organize dad-student sports night, plus line-up dads to provide security checks, grilling for special events, assisting in PE, the library book fair, chorus set building and the like. Over the years of volunteering, I have been able to develop relationships with a lot of dads at the school and then see them around the community. On more than one occasion, a dad has come up to me while out in the community and said, "you're that school dad guy, right." We then strike up a conversation and the conversation soon turns to what I do when I am not at the school; a pastor, and then I can easily turn the corner to spiritual encouragement and extend an invitation to our church. Now, years later as my son continues to attend, this is a routine program I still coordinate. In fact, as I write this, I am just returning from the school where I helped during a required "shelter in place" drill, and then picked up signup forms from two dads wanting to get involved in WATCH D.O.G.S.

Not too many weeks into that first school year, the assistant principal asked if I would be willing to serve on the S.A.C. – the School Advisory Committee. The SAC is a team each Federal Title One school is required to have. Comprised of administration, teachers, parents, and community members, SAC helps to oversee certain federal expenditures and school improvement strategies. I was happy to serve figuring I could be a part of shaping and enhancing my daughter's education. My participation eventually grew to chairing this team for several years as my son Elijah proceeded through each grade.

When I was beginning my second year on SAC, the principal approached me to see if I would be interested in serving on PAC – the Parent Advisory Council. (I know, the acronyms are mind-numbing). Since the commitment to PAC was only three meetings a year, I agreed and continued to do for the next five years. PAC is a *district* level team where parents representing all Title I schools in the county gather to collaborate and influence education and programming. At each meeting we heard what other schools were doing to encourage parent involvement and enhance learning and, what frustrations they were experiencing. We were then tasked to report back what we discussed then take to our school to evaluate. (Side note: This type of partnership and collaboration has helped to make our school district one of the top performing districts in Florida, even though we are one of the lowest funded). Similar to SAC, PAC provided a platform where I could meet parents from across the county who I would then see at community events, grocery store, ball games and the like. What is more, at every meeting, we introduced ourselves and had opportunity to share a bit what we did outside of the school thus giving me more opportunities to have kingdom conversations. Another small way to lay the ground work for bigger impact.

During this time of growing opportunities at the school and district, our church had already launched our benevolence ministry and the Cold Weather Shelter; therefore, we were already beginning to have our foot in the door of the poverty community. (It was through the SAC and PAC that I discovered that free and reduced lunch recipients was the primary measuring stick for federal dollars for Title I schools.) I quickly noticed that many of the families we were seeing in our church ministry were also needing assistance at the school level.[22] Subsequently,

---

[22] If you are in a smaller sized community, less than 30,000, you will frequently see the same people cross over into different sectors of the community, thus opening more ministry

we were becoming positioned to bless and influence families on both fronts. By having a foothold in both, our church was then able to better work with guidance counselors, administrators, teachers and others to more fully connect with families in our community – physically and spiritually. Ministry in this context is not always smooth sailing. There are some times that you must go through heartbreak in order to get to future successes. But we should expect this.

When Jesus sent out the disciples, He sent them out as sheep among wolves (Matthew 10). When Paul the Apostle was writing to the church in Corinth, he gave a resume of pain he endured (2 Corinthians 11). And in his letter to Timothy you see the heartbreak over those who abandoned him (2 Timothy 3). Jesus too felt abandoned by those He counted on most at His time of need, when they fell asleep and then abandoned Him (Luke 22). His Father, of too pure eyes than to behold evil (Habakkuk 1), turned His back on Him while He hung on the cross and our sin hung on Him (Matthew 27). Heartache and frustration are part of the fabric of the uniform of ministry.

Several years ago a single mom, loosely connected through our bus ministry, came into some legal trouble. The Department of Children and Families (DCF) became involved and an investigator became a frequent guest in her home. After the ups and downs of that situation concluded (and may I say

opportunities. Consequently, if you connect with them in one area, it will give you a foothold of ministry to step into another.

that was an extremely painful journey), I had forged a good connection with the DCF investigator and caseworker. When I was at the school doing my volunteer thing, I sometimes saw her come through to deal with a separate circumstance and we would catch up. I would see her at court and other places where I happened to be carrying out the ministry duty of the day and would say, "hi." Before I knew it, she would call our office looking to see if we could help her with a case or at least point her in the right direction. Because she knew my and our church's past work with those in poverty, and the spirit in which we conducted ourselves, she began to trust our counsel. In fact, as I was writing this chapter, we received a call from her seeking our counsel for a single father on the verge of homelessness. So, get this, DCF contacting the church for guidance on how to fulfill a need. (Wild, right?) In that same light, we have also learned of other community organizations that serve struggling families who encourage them to attend our church services because of our reputation to love what many only see as "the least of these." I'm so proud of our church. Again, the community inviting the unchurched to our church. Wild!!

Chip Fox is the Director of Missions for the Santa Rosa Baptist Association. In early 2009, Chip shared with me a new organization called S.A.F.E.R. Santa Rosa. S.A.F.E.R. (Support Alliance For Emergency Readiness), established after hurricanes Ivan and Dennis hit our area, was formed to ensure the county was prepared for, and ready to respond if and when a disaster, such as a hurricane or health crisis, hits our area. Since I recently completed leading the reorganization of our association, Chip asked that I serve on this board to help establish its structure, strategy, etc. By serving on S.A.F.E.R. Santa Rosa, I was able to meet great people from across every sector of our county – law enforcement, government, business, nursing homes, veterans' affairs, and more. It was through these relationships our church was quickly growing better positioned to minister to our members and guests. For instance, when our folks are in the middle of encouraging or discipling someone, they often uncover some type of physical barrier the person is experiencing– legal uncertainty, care for an aging loved one, health concerns, etc. As is often said, "It's not what you know but who you know." Because of our partnership and intentionality to reach out beyond the walls of our campus, our community relationships can point members and guests to the right person or organization in our community that can help them overcome their barriers – thus allowing us to supply holistic guidance. The connection between church and community grew to be a vital partnership that we continue to cherish. Thus, our community is able to support endeavors that our church is engaged in, and we are able to assist our community.

For example, SAFER was applying for our county to be deemed a "Safe Community" by the National Safety Council. Such a designation could be a great bonus for the tourism industry and companies and employees considering moving to our area. To finalize the certification, evaluators were brought in to tour our county and its various sectors – school, law enforcement, tourism, etc. Our church decided to rent the vehicle for the evaluators to use while in town. It only cost us about seventy-five dollars but it made our church proud to play a part in blessing our county, and our county was grateful. What is more, Santa Rosa was awarded the "Safe Community" distinction with one evaluator commenting that one of the strengths of our county is the partnership between the church and the community. A definite kingdom win.

Daniel serves as the day to day coordinator of SAFER. When he was stepping off the Board of Directors for another organization, ESCAROSA Coalition on the Homeless- a dual county organization between Escambia and Santa Rosa County Florida geared to *prevent* homelessness and to serve those who *are* homeless- he recommended the opening to me. With our church's influence growing with the homeless in the county through the Cold Weather Shelter and clothing distribution, we were becoming positioned to begin shaping what was happening on a regional level. Though my schedule prevented me from serving beyond two years, I formed and deepened some great relationships that I have continued to value, and with people like Karen, who have helped our church further the gospel call in some very practical ways.

In 2012, Dr. Karen Barber, the head of the PAC for the school district and fellow board member for the ESCAROSA Coalition on the Homeless, let me know of a speaker who was coming to our city to lead a three-day training to address how to lead families out of generational poverty. Since much of the mission field around our campus consisted of such families, I chose to attend. Bridges out of Poverty, the name of the training program, was the national organization behind the training. Over eighty people attended the training from every sector of our county—faith-based, military, judicial, school, healthcare and more. This training, in line with our biblical mandate to assist "the least of these", ignited the idea of what we could do to address poverty if we really worked together.

A new organization was launched, Santa Rosa Bridges Inc., and I served on the board to get the organizational ball rolling. A key part of Santa Rosa Bridges is hosting "Getting Ahead in a Just Getting by World." This thirteen-week class equips families in poverty with the resources (emotional resources, spiritual resources, physical resources, etc.) to move out of their current situation. These classes are hosted in area churches which provide meals and childcare for the students. When Ferris Hill hosted the class, we recruited a weekly host who prayed with families and a Sunday school class which provided the meal. At the time I am writing this, seventy-seven people have graduated from seven different "Getting Ahead" (GA) classes and over 100 people are on the waiting list.

Hearing the stories of several GA students, I discovered how the lack of transportation was preventing them from climbing out of poverty. Knowing the vast number of churches with vehicles that often go unmoved the majority of the time, I began to wonder how the churches in our area could leverage their transportation resources to serve this "immovable" need.

Before I go any further, I need to clarify something. I do not view myself as any sort of community organizer. That is neither my calling nor my goal. My ongoing desire, for myself and our church, is to find relevant physical "bridges" that will ultimately lead to spiritual destinations- practical areas of ministry that will give opportunity for gospel sharing and biblical kingdom influence. For instance, how volunteering in your child's school could open the door to pray with teachers, administration and parents and share the gospel with them. In this case, I viewed that the need for transportation held the potential for a great outreach opportunity for all our churches. For example, if you picked someone up to take them to a doctor's appointment, you would have a captive audience with whom you could share the gospel and pray with, thus addressing their current physical need and more importantly their eternal spiritual need. Back to transportation.

Two months before the three-day training that led to the forming of Santa Rosa Bridges, the county suspended its two-year trial run of a public transportation program. Since there was no one who could be a voice for those who desperately needed it, the program was parked. Fast forward three years and the need for transportation still existed. It actually grew. But now our churches and community were working together on behalf of the impoverished. Through our efforts with city and county leaders, we were able to get a limited transportation program up going again.   Additionally, several of our local churches now partner together and are on the cusp of using church vehicles and member's personal vehicles to help those in need of transportation get to doctor's appointments.

Consider the "butterfly flaps" I just shared. I began by wanting to be a good dad and serve in my daughter's school.   That one step led to another opportunity that led to another person, which led to another organization and another and another.   My initial step in a kindergarten classroom led to helping to influence and shape what was happening across the county.   That's a process only God could ordain. It's the, "As you go make disciples" part of our faith that God was helping orchestrate.   Consequently, when either our church or I need to address an issue in our community or county, area leaders have responded positively because they have seen our efforts to work for the good of the city – without compromising biblical truth or denying our faith. Even our county's health department nominated us for an award we received from the Governor of Florida for our service to the community.[23]

This effort to become a Kingdom influence in our county took a long time and is still a work in progress. And I have no idea what's next. My initial

---

[23] In October 2015, Ferris Hill was honored and humbled to receive the *Champions of Hope Award* from the office of Florida Governor Rick Scott. Humorously, we received the notification when my new ministry assistant was in her second week. The call shook her for a bit, and I initially thought she took a bad message. Oops.

aim was not to step into shaping government and local issues through biblical principles. My aim was to be a godly dad to my little girl. Even though that one step opened up many doors, our church and myself still remain committed to my initial goal – being the church wherever we are.

What is an opportunity that you could step into in order to live out your faith? What are physical "bridges" around you that could lead to spiritual destinations? Perhaps it is spending an hour a week volunteering at a Pregnancy Resource Center. Maybe it is listening to kids read at a nearby school. Or maybe it is just as simple as sending emails or note cards to area leaders letting them know you are praying for them. You might consider helping coach a community ball team or assisting as a band parent. Whatever it may be, seize it. And as you are in the middle of that opportunity, maximize it. Pray: "Lord, what can I do to bring heaven to earth in this setting? What can I do to be your hands and feet here? Show me how to best be an ambassador of heaven in this corner of our community with *these* people at *this* moment." And then be ready for additional open doors God brings to your obedience. But do not sit around and wait for the next *big* opportunity. The next opportunity God brings you might be as quiet as a butterfly wing.

To Consider

1. What is an opportunity in your community that you could do?

2. What is something you are currently doing where you need to put on "kingdom eyes?"
3. What is an event or organization you are participating in within in your community that you could connect to what your church is doing?
4. Drive around your community, praying that God would show you where He wants you to join Him in what He is doing?

CHAPTER 8
DROP ZONE

"and He made from one man every nation of mankind to live on all the face of the earth, having determined their appointed times and the boundaries of their habitation." –Acts 17:26

The Apostle Paul spoke these words during his Mars Hill sermon in Athens. As he was pointing out the complexity and confusion of their spirituality, he informed them of God's sovereignty. God determines when and where people live. This truth about God's sovereignty, specifically concerning humanity, cannot be forgotten when considering pastoring a church, leading a class or ministry, or engaging the surrounding community or a distant people group. God is intentional.

Military paratroopers have drop zones. Drop zones are predetermined areas where military personnel and resources are to be placed in order to accomplish the mission. These drop zones are not determined in the air when someone looks out the window and shouts, "looks good to me." Instead, planning, preparation and purpose have all been considered when determining the optimal drop zone.

Operation Varsity was a successful airborne forces operation launched by Allied troops that took place toward the end of World War II on March 24, 1945. Involving more than 16,000 paratroopers and several thousand aircraft, *Operation Varsity* was the largest airborne operation in history to be conducted on a single day and in one location. Key to the success of this mission was hitting the strategic drop zones scattered throughout the battlefield. Though each drop zone had its unique landscape, each had its purpose, and each fit into the overall mission.

Similarly, God has placed each of us in strategic drop zones: time, in the 21st century; location, country, state, city; hillside, the particular ministry setting of both home and church campus. These are issues that you had little to no control over. You could not pick what year you would be born or the country or state. And though God has given us free choice, God still maintains His sovereignty over your current address and ministry setting. All that being said, you are where you are right now for a purpose.

Because of God's precision of landing us in a specific drop zone, it behooves us to prayerfully ask, "why am *I* here", "why am I *here*" and "why am I here *right now*?" I recognize that the full answer to these questions might not come during one morning devotion. But these questions are good for you to prayerfully reflect on by taking a 30,000 foot survey of your life against what is going on around you. Consider asking the following:

- What appears to be some of the challenges before our church and community?

- What was going on in my church or community before I arrived?

- What gifts and abilities has God placed within me

to address these issues?

- Of all the times when these areas could be addressed, why now?

- Whose counsel do I value who could show me how my personality meshes with our ministry?

Like I wrote in the previous paragraph, you might not get the full answers to these questions when you might desire, but they will come at the perfect timing. Paul wrote to his protégé Timothy of God's commitment to give understanding (2 Timothy 2:7). But in these quiet unknowns, these gaps of uncertainty, we are still to hold great confidence that God landed us precisely in the drop zone He intended. He was not off target, and He did not send the wrong person.

Every pastor has struggled with their place in ministry. There are days that come when the only thing that holds you there are the books in your office. You consider making a motion at a business meeting to see if the church would permit you to work from home, or on a Caribbean island sharing your sermon via Skype. These moments of emotional and weariness are doors of opportunity that Satan loves to get a foot in.

In these times of uncertainty as to why we are where we are, in life and in ministry, let me encourage you to see them as opportunities to deepen our relationship with God (which is really the main thing all along). If God were to give pastors and ministry leaders the full details of why they are where they are, there would be a greater tendency to focus on the accomplishment of a stated task instead of the pursuit of following and abiding in Him. When the wandering children of Israel woke each day, manna[24] laid outside their tents. The provision was only for the day. Further, they stayed in one location until the "smokey" glory of God shifted. In both situations, they never made plans for the future; rather, they made it a habit of daily looking to God for sustenance and guidance. Sometimes, our attitude reflects the children of Israel a little too much because we spend our time grumbling instead of trusting.

This doesn't mean that where you are right now is permanent. Paul the Apostle had different ministry settings. Jesus and the Twelve ministered in numerous settings. The great commission centered on the gospel moving, being carried by "beautiful feet" (Mt. 28; Rom. 10). But wherever you are, it is a place to be redeemed, a place for God's name to go forth louder and brighter, even if others don't initially see it and you don't always feel it.

During my second Sunday at Ferris Hill, the air conditioner in the worship center acted up. (Not a good thing to happen in humid Florida). We called a contractor who came out the next day to fix it. The contractor was a great Christian business owner in our community who had a long relationship with and knowledge of Ferris Hill. I still remember him

---

[24] Manna literally means, "what's this?"

stopping by my office that day. We chatted for a moment about a few of the HVAC needs of the facility. He then shared with me a little more history of the church that I did not know. Finally, with a compassionate yet concerned look on his face, he asked me, "What are you doing here?" Though he might not have intended to communicate this, what I strongly felt he was saying was, "this place just needs to be crossed off the list. There are better places where you could be used. So what are you doing here?"

I have to admit those comments did give me a moment of pause. I was aware that the journey ahead looked like a long and uphill climb (though longer and steeper than I knew then), but I could not dismiss the hand of God in bringing me there. For example, I had no idea how the search team got my résumé. Next, the home we owned in Pensacola sold the afternoon we accepted the call to be pastor, before we could even put it on the market. Additionally, as I had walked through the building on my first day, I saw some pictures of previous pastors hanging on a wall and discovered that my childhood pastor was the first pastor of the church when it started as a mission over fifty years earlier. These were but three examples, plus dozens more that would follow, where God reminded me, "I'm in this. I got you here for such a time as this. I have placed you in the middle of my drop zone. Trust me."

These reminders are helpful during days of struggle. Even though there is excitement in having a front row seat to the revitalization of a church, it doesn't mean the drop zone God placed you in will mean you won't land in mud. A couple of challenges multiply into ten. People discover their spiritual gift of criticism or complacency. You realize the bullets flying at you are "friendly." Discouragement and doubt want to become tenants in the rooms of your mind. Mud is dirty. Thorns are painful. Climbing hills is tiring. They were for Jesus, too.

A recurring question that shapes my pastorate is, what would Jesus do in this situation? To answer that question, I have to regularly, often daily, visualize myself from His perspective. Not always comfortable, usually not. He never got what He deserved. He gave what was undeserved. The greatest struggles He faced were with those who were religious. Those He counted on did not follow through, and even fell asleep at a needed prayer meeting. The struggle of the moment, though not fully understood by onlookers, paved the way for the long-term, eternal good.

The "Jesus perspective" on pastoring inspires me to plow through the mud, thorns, and hills. I intentionally pursue to view benevolence situations like Jesus demonstrated benevolence in His incarnation and atonement. I viewed meetings and strategy development like a shepherd giving guidance and nurture to his sheep, instead of a CEO to his subordinates. By and large, letting the attitude be in me that was also in Christ Jesus (Phil 2:5) gives me great patience as I remember this is about revitalizing people, flawed people, with a flawed leader, me, and not merely rebuilding an organization as quick as possible.

The "Jesus perspective" probably went through Titus's mind also. One of my favorite pastoral passages is found in Paul's letter to Titus. In the first chapter Paul tells Titus the reason for his ministry,

> *"For this reason I left you in Crete, that you would set in order what remains and appoint elders in every city as I directed you,"*

Paul was intentionally leaving Titus in a place that had disorder so that he might "set in order" – even those the locals referred to as "rebellious men, empty talkers and deceivers" (1:10). Can't you hear Titus asking, "What am I doing here?"

Recognizing that God has "dropped" you where you are with intention will necessitate regular personal evaluation. I need to ask, and continue to ask, and answer the following questions: Since God has me in this church right now, and in this community right now, to lead and influence these people, how well am I letting God lead and influence me? What adjustments in my character must be made and maintained? Who has God placed in my life, both inside and outside my ministry context, who can help accomplish what God is requiring?

For pastors, think back to the day God led the church to call you to be their pastor or staff member. For lay ministry leaders, think back to the day God led the pastor or other church leader to ask you to take the helm of a class or ministry. God didn't just call *someone* to a ministry position. He called *you* to a ministry position. Of the 7.3 billion people in the world, only you have that position. Anyone in the world could occupy that chair of opportunity, but you are the only one God has ordained to do so. Though a child might hear a certain biblical account a thousand times during their life, you get to tell it to them for the first time. Such a thought is a reminder that there are no small positions in the kingdom of God. All of us are vital. And it requires that every day we wake up praying,

> "Lord, you placed *me* here, for this moment in time, for *this* church, *this* ministry, *these* people and *this* community. Guide me to redeem this day using the skills and gifts you have given me, for Your glory and to accomplish your purposes."

Before I wrap up this chapter, let me share one more idea that has helped me. Struggling to answer the "why am I here" question often comes because we spend all our time staring exclusively and extremely up close to the "trees" in our current ministry and not taking time to discover the entire "forest" of God's kingdom. As I read, learn, and encounter what is happening in other churches, and especially around the world in life-threatening ministry environments that many of our brothers and sisters in Christ endure, I glean strength for the environment I am in. I often think, "What do I have to complain about? This is no big deal. I'm being petty. They are literally willing to take a bullet, I'm struggling with a complaint. They sojourn on in the face of terrorist threats, I have no reason to slow down." So in case you might not feel a tremendous burden to rely on the word and ministry of this pastor from the Panhandle of Florida, look to your brothers and sisters around the world and remember that God has placed you where you are for a purpose. You got this – for such a time as this. Better yet, He's got you.

"Consider it all joy, my brethren, when you encounter various trials, knowing that the testing of your faith produces endurance. And let endurance have its perfect result, so that you may be perfect and complete, lacking in nothing" James 1:2-4 NASB.

To Consider

1. What abilities and gifts has God given you that are uniquely appropriate for your ministry setting?
2. If Jesus were the pastor of your church, what are one or two items He would do immediately?
3. Where could you go to learn, or who could you meet with, in order to learn what ministry is like in difficult settings around the world?

CHAPTER 9
PASTOR'S EYES ONLY (OR WHOEVER ELSE WANTS TO LOOK)

One of the few television shows I'll stop for a couple of minutes to watch is *American Pickers*. For those who haven't seen the show, it is a mixture, in my opinion, between *Antique Roadshow* and *Hoarders*. The two hosts travel America looking through collectors' junk (oops, I mean priceless collectibles) to see what treasures are buried. They purchase them for a deal to later resale them for a profit. The thrust of the show is the sorting through the junk (again, oops) to find the treasure. But *American Pickers* could be remade into *American Pastors*.

There are treasures galore within the pastorate:

- Seeing the person far from God step over the line of faith and receive forgiveness;

- Having a front row seat to couples united in holy matrimony or restored after a season of struggle;

- Observing the transforming power a Spirit-empowered body of faith can have upon the surrounding community.

The list is long. I'm sure you could make one. But there is also the junk.

Take a moment and think of all the junk that one experiences in the church. One person wants to financially contribute to ministries or projects of their personal preferences, not the "General Fund." Everyone wants you to "scratch their itch." The facility is wearing and crumbling. The sermon is too long (yours not mine). People try to condone their sexual misconduct. Commitments are not kept. Divorce. Death. Sickness. Last minute requests. Promises broken, excuses abundant. Priorities unholy misplaced. Such junk, and thousands more like these, is inevitable. They are inevitable because we are in a fallen world with sinful, though redeemed, people, including the pastor at the helm. There are times when the pastor feels he is spending all of his time searching through the junk in order to find the treasure. Though we have been able to see revitalization at Ferris Hill, it has not been glamorous. Let me take a moment and share some of the junk.

Building and Grounds

When I arrived as pastor, little had been done to the facility in many years. Besides a quick fix of the roof and worship center walls after a hurricane, much of the facility had been unkept. Though mostly clean, there were years of clutter in the corners of every room. The red shag carpet in the student center was well-worn. The gas supply line for our heater system was spliced several times.[25] Mold was growing on

---

[25] We nicknamed one unit "back-draft" as it blew massive flames when being re-lit. On one occasion it singed the eyebrows of a deacon.

ceiling tiles from the stale air. The pre-school and worship areas had a lingering dirt smell from the return-air supply being pulled through a partially collapsed underground system. The gas water heater for the baptistery, located in a women's restroom, had no vent thus building up dangerous carbon monoxide levels when turned on. The boiler system that conditioned half the facility air had all the safety valves bypassed. Long wood-paneled hallways were lit by a single bulb, with the light switch located in the middle of the hallway. Abandoned electrical wires were laying in the ceiling though electricity still ran to them. And I haven't even mentioned the outside yet, or the leaking roof, or the sixty year old windows, or clogged and collapsed drain lines.[26] Found the treasure?

Tackling these obstacles, plus seemingly endless more, were not moments that I treasured. They were painful and frustrating and aggravating and tiring. But part of the treasure was that we didn't have any debt. We were obligated to no one except ourselves and God, and the mission He had for us. As we tackled each item that surfaced, sometimes like a whale blowing forth its spew, we were able to make adjustments so that our facility was a better tool God could use to accomplish what He was asking us to do. We felt each room was a canvas that needed to be painted according to the blueprint God had for us. Subsequently, a choir room turned into a clothes

---

[26]In 2008 we accomplished a five year renovation project in 52 days following the book of Nehemiah. We called it "the Nehemiah Project." We finished with fifteen minutes to spare before our celebration service.

closet, a storage area turned into Sunday School headquarters, extra space turned into a multi-purpose area, clutter moved out and areas for discipleship and ministry moved in.

I wish I could write to tell you that the revitalization of our facility is complete. But with the ministry resource of a sixty plus year old facility, the work is never done. We currently need our bathrooms need to be expanded to ensure those who are disabled have ease of access. This is just one example of ongoing work of revitalization that involve a long-standing facility. But we have a facility as a resource for corporate worship and ministry! And perhaps you do as well. Be thankful for that. You don't have to set up and take down each week. Unlike many church planters, you don't have to deal with school guidelines if you rent a space on campus. Whatever the facility is that God has given you, view it as a treasure. Sure it might need some scrubbing and fixing, but so do the people who attend. If broken windows and cracked walls and cluttered rooms concern you, you are in good company. Nehemiah had concerns for the broken walls of Jerusalem. But he inspected and prayed and led a monumental rebuilding effort. You can too.

Issues of poverty, homelessness, drugs, and jail

Jesus knew what He was talking about when He said, "the poor will always be among you." (Of course He did). It's not a coincidence that the poor being "among you" is closely connected with our responsibility to minister to "the least of these."

Serving the struggling and needy in the name of Jesus is an essential way we live out our faith. This doesn't mean it will be easy.

As I write, I am finishing up an intense, yet sadly normal, morning of assisting our benevolence team as they distributed food and clothing and spiritual encouragement. I came down to our welcome area to counsel some benevolence guests who were homeless – a 19 year old recently released from prison along with his 18 year old female friend. At the adjacent table was a 20 year old who was looking for a job and housing guidance while his girlfriend was around the corner from our campus at the Pregnancy Resource Center. After them, a couple came who lived in a camper 200 yards from our campus but had absolutely nothing and was being forced to relocate in five days. Finally, a woman I have worked with off and on over the years came seeking help as her husband was just sentenced to prison. She had just received an eviction notice, her car insurance had lapsed, and her tag was to be renewed the following week on her birthday. She was due in court in a neighboring county in three days for failure to pay a speeding ticket and didn't know if she would be arrested when she arrived. Whew! Needless to say, it was a busy morning.

When we "be the church", and as we pastor those who "be the church", we will have many days like this. I contend that such days will only increase in the days ahead as brokenness appears to be on the rise in every corner of our culture. It's in these moments your heart can get heavy, your mind can grow numb, and the gauges on your emotional limits can max out.

Junk. Yet we need to be wise that we don't let the junk around us begin to rust our hearts and corrode our minds. There is treasure.

With the brokenness on the rise, people are more open to listening. They are seeking hope, and there is no better source for hope than the gospel of Jesus Christ. They are looking for guidance, and there is no greater wisdom than that found in God's word of the Bible, instilled by His Holy Spirit. While we continue to engage the community around us on *their* turf, I can see that just opening the doors of the church and opening our hearts so that we treat others the way Christ treated us has an eternal impact. But treasurers often are still covered in soot.

Our staff has the website to the county "jail view" saved on our computers and phones. Rarely does a week go by when we do not discover or someone does not direct us to someone we recently ministered to, a parent of one of the children in our ministry, or even a church member who is still experiencing the effects of decisions made before they met Christ or struggling to "crucify the flesh." I have kidded with our folks that we minister to those in a nearby gated community – the local jail. When picking classes at seminary, I never saw an option for "ministry in the criminal justice system." But for me to evangelize and disciple in our mission field, I had to become familiar with the judicial "point system", local jail to state prison guidelines, various legal steps and the like. And I'll be the first to admit, it's frustrating to see a guy being attentive and engaged in worship on Sunday and then needing to visit him in jail the following week. If you seek to revitalize your church and do so by ministering to "the least of these" that surround you, you need to prepare yourself for this type of mess.[27] The mess is the real world that millions of people in our country nearly drown in every day.

A key way that I have survived over a decade of this ministry is seeing myself in their position. Christ Jesus saw me in the middle of my mess. He stepped out of the comfort of Heaven, surrounded by the resources of Heaven, and offered compassion, healing, guidance, mercy and hope. He gave me a future. That's what we try to do for those in our church and community. Those who are swimming in the junk don't see a future for themselves. They are just trying to make it through the day. But the gospel breaks through the moment and gives them an eternal perspective.

Let me be clear, my job, our church's job, is NOT to merely be a case worker for social issues. Holiness is our goal, not just getting someone in a home. Feasting on the Bread of Life is our goal, not just filling the belly for a moment. But assisting in housing and filling the belly are bridges we can walk across with someone to lead them to the eternal goal. Can we always help? No. I say "no" more than I say "yes." Many times, I can only reply, "Silver and gold have I none, but what I can give you is eternal life"

---

[27] A quick glance in the Hall of Faith of Hebrews 11 will show you the depth of mess one can go through in the journey of following God.

(Acts 3:6). If they turn it down, so be it. But I know that I have done my absolute best at reflecting the character of Jesus and obeying what He says His followers are to do as ambassadors of reconciliation.

Multiple generations

According to those who analyze culture, there are primarily five generations among us today - the "Greatest", the Boomers, the Generation Xers, the Millennials, and Generation Z. If you are fortunate, your church will have a healthy representation of each. But if you have been in the pastorate more than five minutes, you know that four generations don't always agree on how church and ministry life should be lived. One prefers a certain expression of music and another embraces another view on the priority of missions. Because the pastor is often the one who hears the thoughtful concerns (who am I kidding, "complaints"), there can be a temptation to focus on the differences among us and then organize toward those ends. If fully pursued, a church will end up with everyone in their generational corners doing church according to their personal desires.

For churches under 200, this form of generational-driven ministry puts immense strain upon the resources of the church (financial, people, etc.). Sustaining independent yet meaningful ministry for each generation is a challenge. Further, fragmentation becomes much more apparent compared to churches in larger settings. We cannot afford everyone retreating to their preferential corners.

But instead of seeing the differences between the generations, the church pursuing revitalization should focus on that which unites them. The beginning point is the Bible. All generations are of one faith, guided by one Word, heading for one eternal destination. (On a side note: if we are going to spend eternity together, let's start loving and enjoying each other now.) Next is the unity and commonality found in the family. Older generations are more open to engaging and embracing younger generations when they see their children and grandchildren are part of those "other" generations, asking questions such as, "what could we do as a church, in our methodology or music or ministry, to reach your children, grandchildren, and their friends?" Likewise, looking to the younger generations, we can ask, "what can we do to learn from and grow from the wisdom of the generations who have come before us? What can we do to reach your mom or dad?" It's when these questions are asked and answered that people move from their generational corners and are much more willing to meet together as a united body, all working toward a kingdom goal.

Fewer people

When ministry is done, it is done through people. When ministries are added, either the responsibility is given to new people or it is added on top of the current responsibilities of those already serving. In the smaller-sized church there are fewer people to either give to or add to. Now I fully realize that ministry is proportional. Medium to mega-size church leaders would say they too feel the number of those able and willing to take ministry responsibilities is limited. Ministry is proportional. I get that. I hear you, and I have been there. But when crunching the actual numbers, small churches have fewer people and thus a smaller pool of possibilities. Subsequently, a higher percentage of people must "pull their weight." Additionally, when those who hold responsibility fail to follow through or step down, the Pastor has less options and can feel the load more quickly and directly. He doesn't always have a staff to whom he can say, "fix it", or a sufficient deacon body who he can turn to and say, "fill the need", and then go about his business. While the numbers in the small church might be fewer, the size of the mission field remains the same. The pastor leading the church of 150 can have the same, or even greater, burden for the community as the pastor only a couple miles away who is leading a church of 1000. It's a burden. But the same power of the Holy Spirit that raised Jesus from the dead is in both – that's the treasure.

Essential to serve; imperative to pray

Pastors of all churches, both small and large, should set the example of a servant. Philippians 2 shouts the call for us to have this attitude like Jesus did, and we should lead our church in this endeavor. Toward this end, work hard. I mean work really hard. I mean get sweaty and give it all you've got. But before you do, be sure your efforts are fueled by prayer and not just your innate personal drive. Looking back on my pastoral journey thus far, I stressed and modeled service yet regrettably did little to set the tone in prayer. I would often lay out a strategy and pursue to execute it praying for strength along the way. I now look back and see huge gaps that were missed and the impact that was reduced because I prayed *after* the fact. I was rushing for the accomplishment of a task, instead of walking in stride with the Holy Spirit.

Through prayer, clarity is given. Through prayer, order is given. Through prayer, timing is given. Through prayer, you know when to push "pause" on a ministry or task. Through prayer, you know when to push forward.

In 2013 our church raised the level of prayer in our church – corporate praying, small group praying, online praying, prayer days, prayer rooms, and much more. Through this increase, we feel God at work. And let me say, it is nice to have a sense that God is working even when you take a moment to be still.

Rest

I am not good at rest. Actually, I'm lousy. While I usually get everything done in the day that I plan to, I pack my days down to the minute. My sleep schedule is nothing to emulate.

For years, I have felt guilty for taking a moment to sit still for thirty minutes and do something for myself – watch a game, take a nap, or (I actually can't even think of anything). It has been common for me to go a couple of years without a vacation except a day here or a half-day there. Not wise. I still have not fully figured out rest and relaxation out. Recently, I actually spent some time *studying* rest, and even scheduling rest. When the scheduled time came, I worked hard at "resting" but was restless every second. But slowly, and I mean slowly, I am discovering that proper rest is godly and is needed.

For the pastor pursuing revitalization in his church, learning to rest will be essential. If you do, enjoying those around you will be easier. You will have patience with those who you would rather ignore. You will be able to walk the extra mile when your weariness would tempt you to walk away. If you don't, carpool buddies you call Frustration and Burnout will ride with you every day to the office.

I don't know what rest feels like to you, but figure it out. Discover what are some things to do in your community and experience them. Take a nap. Turn your phone off. Delete some apps. Wait a day to return an email. Your church will not collapse. You are not that important. God's got this. He's got you. It's okay. Rest.

This chapter is not exhaustive by any stretch. My goal in sharing it is to let you know that I feel your pain. Revitalization is not easy. It is messy. It is tiring. But it is possible. You are not alone in what you are trying to do even though most days you feel like the only one in the world doing anything. When those days come, remember my name. I feel your pain. And then, *turn your eyes upon Jesus, look full in His wonderful face, and the things of earth will grow strangely dim, in the light of His glory and grace.*[28]

To Consider

1. Write down three messy items you have experienced in this ministry setting (either categorical or specific example)?
2. How has God used those messes to teach you about Himself? About yourself? About the people or community you minister to?
3. If you were to go back and do that situation again, how would you do it differently (consider physical, attitude, spiritual factors?)
4. Based off those lessons you have now learned, is there a current situation you could apply your lesson to before it becomes a mess?

---

[28] Turn Your Eyes Upon Jesus was written by Helen Lemmel

CONCLUSION
BE the CHURCH

If you have made it to this page of our story, I thank you. There have been times along the way of *living* this story that I wanted to stop "writing" it. Further, I wish I could tell you that our story of revitalization is complete; however, until we cross heaven's welcome mat and see Jesus face to face, there is still much work to do – we still look so unlike Jesus, and so does our community. Additionally, at each step of our journey we have sensed Satan nipping at our heals always seeking to steal, kill and destroy our revitalization – what God has enlivened, Satan desires to deaden. We take nothing for granted.

There have been moments when thoughts of doubt have crept in my mind. In these moments, and; at times, seasons, I only trust in the comforting words of Christ Jesus, "You will do Greater things..." and "the gates of hell will not prevail..."[29] Thus, I trust them fully, and I take another step. I'm still here on this earth, thus, God has more for me to do, and He has more for our church to do. The same is true for you and your church. If you are doubting and struggling, look to the words of your Savior. Rest in them. And then take another step – in HIS strength. There's greater things still to be done.

I ask that you pray for us and know that I am praying for you and your church.

---

[29] John 14:12; Matthew 16:18

God of This City[30]

You're the God of this city
You're the King of these people
You're the Lord of this nation
You are

You're the Light in this darkness
You're the Hope to the hopeless
You're the Peace to the restless
You are

There is no one like our God
There is no one like our God

For greater things have yet to come
And greater things are still to be done in this city
Greater thing have yet to come
And greater things are still to be done in this city

BEtheCHURCH

---

[30] God of the City was written by Aaron Boyd, often performed by Chris Tomlin

APPENDIX 1
Battle Buddy Check-Up

Questions to Start:
1. What can we celebrate? How has God blessed you?
2. What problem has consumed your thoughts this week?

Spiritual Life:
1. God's Word: How consistent were you in spending time in God's word this past week? What has God been teaching you?
2. Prayer: Describe your prayers: for yourself and for others.
3. Temptation: How have you been tempted this week? How did you respond? Are there any life adjustments you can make to ease the struggle?
4. Confession: Do you have any unconfessed sin in your life? Are you ready to take time to deal with it now?
5. Worship: Did you worship in church this week? Was your faith in Jesus strengthened? Was He honored in you?
6. Witness: Have taken opportunities to share your faith this past week? In what ways? How can you improve? Who do you feel led to invite to church? to your home?

Home Life:
1. Wife/Husband: How is it going with your spouse (time, meaningful conversation, attitudes, intimacy, irritations, disappointments, her/his relationship with Christ)?
2. Children: How are your children (grandchildren)? Are you giving encouragement, quality/quantity time, spiritually influencing and educating them? How can you strengthen your spiritual influence this next week?
3. Finances: How are your finances doing (debts, sharing, saving, spending, tithing)?
4. Time: How have you invested your time around the house?

Work/Relationship Life:

1. Job/School: How are things going (career progress, relationships, temptations, work load, stress, problems, working too much)?
2. Relationships: Are your current relationships helping you move in the right direction? Any relationships that need to be mended?

Critical Concerns:

1. God's Will: Do you feel you are in the center of God's will? Do you sense His peace?
2. Thought Life: What are you wrestling with in secret?
3. Service: What have you done for someone else this week which can't be repaid?
4. Priorities: Are your priorities in the right order? What adjustments need to happen?
5. Integrity: Is your moral and ethical behavior as it should be?
6. High-Risk: How are you doing in personal high-risk areas?
7. Transparency: is the "visible" you and the "real" you consistent in our relationship? If not, in what ways? (Have you just lied to me?)

Close the check-up praying for each other. Focus on concerns for the upcoming week that have been expressed.

APPENDIX 2
Our Mission Field 1 (Jerusalem)

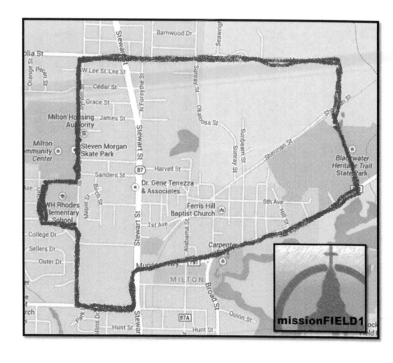

ABOUT THE AUTHOR

Brian and his wife Candace live in Milton, Florida. They have two children, Baleigh and Elijah. Brian graduated from the University of Mobile (B.S., Religion, 1998); and New Orleans Baptist Theological Seminary (M.Div., 2002; D.Min. 2008). He has served in churches in Alabama and Florida.

74603681R00084

Made in the USA
Columbia, SC
06 August 2017